Fine Arts in the Curriculum

D1416387

Fine Arts in the Curriculum

Frederick B. Tuttle, Jr., Editor

nea PROFESSIONAL LIBRARY
National Education Association
Washington, D.C.

GARDNER WEBB COLLEGE LIBRARY

NX
303
.F56
1985

Copyright © 1985
National Education Association of the United States

Note

The opinions expressed in this publication should not
be construed as representing the policy or position of the
National Education Association. Materials published as
part of the Reference & Resource Series are intended to be
discussion documents for teachers who are concerned
with specialized interests of the profession.

Library of Congress Cataloging in Publication Data
Main entry under title:

Fine arts in the curriculum.

   (Reference & resource series)
   Includes bibliographical references.
   1. Arts—Study, and teaching (Elementary)—United
States.   2. Arts—Study and teaching (Secondary)-
United States.   I. Tuttle, Frederick B.   II. Series:
Reference and resource series.
NX303.F56 1985 ·   700'.7'1273   85–8930
ISBN 0–8106–1531–2

CONTENTS

NEA RESOLUTION

B-28. Fine Arts Education

The National Education Association believes that artistic expression is basic to an individual's intellectual, aesthetic, and emotional development and therefore must be included as a component of all education.

The Association urges its state affiliates to become involved in the promotion, expansion, and implementation of a fine arts program in the curriculum of their various local school systems. (80,84)

Chapter 1

WHAT'S IT ALL ABOUT?

Frederick B. Tuttle, Jr.

As I reflect on the issue of fine arts in relation to curriculum development, I realize this is an area that must be an integral part of any comprehensive educational system, yet it is also an area that has been continually relegated to the fringe of most curricula. Through the presentation of this collection of essays I hope to alert educators to the vital role fine arts should play in the total educational process. The aim is for all of us to make concerted efforts to ensure the recognition of the fine arts as both special subjects and as components of general content area subjects.

Like most other curriculum developers and coordinators, over the past few years I have felt a strong need to reexamine all the basic content areas, especially math and science, to meet the demands of excellence in education. This, coupled with the stress on basis skills, testing, and budget cuts, has often kept serious consideration of the fine arts to a minimum. Indeed, as Fowler quotes in "Addressing the Issues: The Case for the Arts," these forces have promoted "the sadly consistent relegation of the arts to the curricular caboose." As the caboose of the curriculum, fine arts classes are sometimes valued mostly as vehicles to gain preparation time for teachers or as elective, frill courses squeezed in between the real courses required for graduation and college admission. Why should it be otherwise, considering the limited time students have to learn reading, math, social studies, science, English, health, physical education, business, industrial arts, home economics, and foreign languages?

We should examine the role of the fine arts in the curriculum because they are directly related to the general goals of education. These goals may be viewed as social, institutional, and individual. As a function of society, one of the major goals of education should be to promote the continuation of culture, transmitting values and concepts of civilization from one generation to the next. One of the major objectives within this goal is to help individuals place themselves into perspective historically and culturally. However, with the explosion of information the best we can aim for in our schools is to help students become capable of gaining, evaluating, and sharing knowledge. In his analysis of the major reports on education (p. 61), Fowler quotes Goodlad:

As part of the process of enculturation, students should "develop an awareness and understanding of

one's cultural heritage and become familiar with the achievements of the past that have inspired and influenced humanity" as well as "learn how to apply the basic principles and concepts of fine arts and humanities to the appreciation of the aesthetic contributions of other cultures."

The aesthetic contribution has often reflected attitudes toward society. A major role of the fine arts in democratic societies has been that of social critic. In a symposium on arts and humanities conducted in 1968, Edgar Friedenberg commented that humanities and arts act "as a 'detector organ' to discover what is wrong with the society".[1] It is vital for individuals in a democratic society to be able to determine influences on their values and to make decisions about whether or not to accept those influences. Schools, then, have a primary obligation to provide students with background and skills to critically evaluate information and influences from a variety of sources, including print, oral, visual, and music media. The ultimate objective is to enable students to make appropriate decisions based on analysis and evaluation of information and alternatives. Instruction in the fine arts helps students acquire these abilities that are, in turn, necessary for productive participation in the democratic process and the preservation of democratic ideals.

As educational institutions, schools have generated a variety of curricula. These curricula, however, have often become fragmented by the variety of demands placed upon school systems. Many educators fear that the current necessary stress on math and science will detract from emphasis on other curricular areas. The weakening of one area, however, will ultimately affect all areas. Efland, in "Excellence in Education: The Role of the Arts," addresses this concern: "The creation of a balanced curriculum is one of the most pressing curriculum problems of the day. . . . [When the arts] are found to be strong, it is likely that the total program has quality as well. Conversely, if strength in the arts is lacking, other parts of the program are probably wanting, for the quality of the arts is a barometer that serves to indicate the levels of economic support for the total school program."

One of the aims of a curriculum is usually to develop student characteristics such as creativity, ability to draw abstractions, ability to analyze and evaluate, and high motivation self-expectations. Yet, we often stifle these characteristics in many standard courses by encouraging students to learn only the knowledge we already possess, to answer the questions to which we already have the correct responses. In many arts classes, however, these characteristics are highly valued. In his essay, "Art, Creativity, and the Quality of Education," Jon Murray, a high school visual arts instructor, states: "Learning to take risks and cope with frustration is an important part of original, creative thinking in any field; in art it is *central* to good instruction. The teacher must relinquish control over the ultimate success of the work and become an understanding guide, a source of encouragement, criticism, and support." The goal of art "is not to make every student an artist, but to exploit art as a unique vehicle for developing the individual creative potential in every student."

Robert Alexander, in "What Are Children Doing When They Create?" relates the value of the creative process for young children: "In the act of creation, children are closer to their truth than at any other time. Children can fully express their humanistic feelings of caring deeply about other people, about nature, about animals, about *life*." This attitude toward instruction and learning should permeate all curricular areas if our graduates are to continue to learn and to produce on their own volition.

Use of the arts in instruction not only provides creative outlets for students but also exposes individuals to alternative modes of acquiring concepts. Moreover, use of the arts in instruction also provides additional opportunities for students to communicate their understandings and feelings to others. Some individuals fall into the mold of the traditional student learning effectively through reading and lectures and demonstrating their understandings adequately on tests and written papers. An increasing number of students, however, possess different learning characteristics and require other means to gain information—usually more visual and experiential—and different avenues through which to express their understandings. Efland echoes this need to address a variety of learning characteristics: "Human intelligence has various ways of forming thought, some of which involve the kinds of images found in the arts. Yet we structure curriculum and teaching as if the arts do not contribute to our ability to understand." When teachers have used the arts in other areas of the curriculum to teach concepts and skills, they have usually been very successful. In "The First Songs of Summer," Steinberg and Traub found that incorporating music with writing enabled learning-disabled students to communicate their ideas effectively in writing.

By incorporating visual arts in content areas I have found many students who have experienced reading difficulty not only learn the concepts more effectively, but also begin to read with greater comprehension. In "Robert's Problem . . . Or Ours?" I concluded:

[Using nonprint media to teach concepts often allows students who have failed in most of their classes to be successful in an academic setting]. . . . This approach [also] helps poor readers use their comprehen-

sion skills more actively and successfully in academic situations, it also provides them with the conceptual background necessary for understanding printed versions of similar ideas. . . . If we can show students how to apply comprehension skills in one medium, we may be able to help them transfer this knowledge and confidence to [printed materials].

The use of a variety of media for instruction not only helps students comprehend ideas, but it also helps them communicate their understandings to others. The inability to communicate in academic environments contributes greatly to the frustrations and poor self-concepts of these individuals. To alleviate this situation, we must provide alternative avenues for students to share their ideas and feelings with others. Often, nonprint media provide these opportunities. When applying a multimedia approach teaching poetry, I found many nonreaders could, indeed, interpret poetry and share their reactions with others. After showing students visual interpretations of poetry and asking them to respond critically to the interpretation, I also found that once they were able to communicate their ideas to others through one medium, they were able to express themselves in writing more effectively. I concluded, "If students have a successful experience with one medium, they may have additional media opened automatically to them. Once the students have found they can read real visual images accompanying a poem, they can read and react critically to the poem itself [in its printed version]" ("Visualizing Poetry," *Media & Methods*, May 1970). Instruction in fine arts and integration of fine arts in other areas of the curriculum strengthen the entire curriculum throughout the school by enabling individuals to participate in the learning process more comfortably and more effectively.

What can we do about establishing and integrating fine arts in the curriculum? First, we must stop "blaming the victim." William Ryan coined this phrase to discuss sociological issues and ways we tend to blame those who are actually victims of society rather than focus attention on the real causes of problems. He cites the following to illustrate the concept:

Twenty years ago Zero Mostel used to do a sketch in which he impersonated a Dixiecrat Senator conducting an investigation of the origins of World War II. At the climax of the sketch, the Senator boomed out, "What was Pearl Harbor *doing* in the Pacific?" (Ryan, *Blaming the Victim*. New York: Random House, 1976)

As Fowler points out, "one of the root problems is fractional bickering and splintering of the profession. . . ." Although he is referring primarily to music, I believe this may be extended to all areas of education. In recent years education has experienced severe criticism, heavy budget cuts, increased instructional demands, and calls for more accountability. In an effort to protect their turf, teachers in many fields of education have blamed their colleagues in other areas of education for the problems. The resulting infighting has fragmented the total educational effort. When faced with severe budgetary constraints, we have often sacrificed some instructional areas to save money for the more vital educational experiences. The victims of these cuts have often been fine arts courses with the justification that these frills are not so important as the basics.

While some of the recent criticism and demands for accountability may be appropriate and deserved, they should not be shouldered by any single area of education. All areas require examination and refinement. One of our major tasks as educators should be to communicate effectively to the public and its representatives. Part of this communication should involve detailed statements of the goals of education and descriptions of how the various areas of education work together to achieve these goals. This need for cooperation and integration is especially vital in the fine arts.

Although many fine arts teachers promote integration with other areas, in reality they often even vie with each other for the crumbs of the school budget. This problem is exemplified in the essays by O'Hara, Logan, and Gensemer as they discuss individual areas of fine arts as separate entities. However, O'Hara concludes, "Drama in education, it would appear, must confine itself to fulfilling only those curriculum roles which it manifestly can be seen to be fulfilling. The most important of these roles is its central curriculum function as a learning process." If we view all areas as part of the total learning process, we can stop blaming the victim and begin working together to focus on the entire learning experience. All areas of education are victims; we must work together to validate the entire educational process in this country.

The second thing we should do is to integrate fine arts into the general curriculum more effectively. While it is important to study the arts as separate fields with unique characteristics, it is equally important to show relationships among all forms of communication and to demonstrate the vital role fine arts can play in other curricular areas. This requires active, continual communication among all teachers. Through continuing dialogue we can focus on areas of the learning process that cross disciplines and promote mutual instruction and reinforcement in those areas.

In some cases this integration will be in content. For example, both visual arts and geometry teachers work with the delineation and derivation of geometric shapes. In other cases the relationship will be in the teaching-learning process. Alexander alludes to the relationship between creativity and cognition—both important processes in all learning. Murray draws relationships between teaching strategies in art and writing, indicating that both visual arts and writing teachers use a "composing process" (Tuttle, 1977 and 1978)[2] approach as students draft, share, evaluate, and redraft works before submission for final evaluation.

The relationship may also be found in the skills being developed albeit in different media. Murray illustrates this relationship between visual arts and science:

One day I discovered a student of mine memorizing biology notes for an upcoming text. I wondered out loud why art and science are taught so differently, since art-making and science-making are essentially the same process. Both, after all, are attempts to investigate and better understand the world by using observation, creative experimentation, and study to produce results.

When fine arts teachers describe what and how they teach, relationships to other areas of education become evident. After tracing the application of performance in literary interpretation in "The Performance of Literature," Hudson and Long "affirm the humanness, even the naturalness, of literary study and the possibilities of insight through literature in performance." "On the Cutting Edge" provides illustrations of potential integration of the arts in other areas as fine arts teachers describe specific lessons and experiences that have direct bearing on social studies and English. In "The Computer in the Fine Arts," Kepner illustrates relationships that can exist between such seemingly disparate areas as fine arts in computer education. The examples he provides not only demonstrate how teachers can use computers to teach some fine arts concepts and skills but also, indirectly, how students can learn computer operation in the process.

In "The Implications for the Arts of Recent Education Studies and Reports," Fowler highlights the need for the integration of fine arts in the school curricular as expressed in the Report of the National Commission on Excellence in Education:

[The Commission] maintains that knowledge of humanities [including the arts] "must be harnessed to science and technology if the latter are to remain creative and humane, just as the humanities [including the arts] need to be informed by science and technology if they are to remain relevant to the human condition."

Finally, to promote the fine arts in the curriculum we must delineate and describe what is learned through the fine arts. As O'Hara notes, "Creative arts teachers, however, while generally subscribing to creative expression as the broad banner philosophy under which they operate, are beginning to realize that highly individualized translations of this philosophy into the different arts subjects are unlikely to stand up to close curriculum scrutiny."

To be sure, "of more importance is the large goal of defining the general role of the arts in education," but the specific components of each area must be delineated before their place in the general curriculum can be effectively described. As we move toward more accountability, teachers will have to be ready and willing to describe what they teach in terms that enable others to determine what students are learning.

As a curriculum coordinator I also look for the development of learning, as sequential building of skills and concepts. Many fine arts experiences are not taken seriously because teachers are not able to explain in concrete terms what students are learning in the courses. While most of us verbally accept fine arts in the curriculum, many outside the arts still consider courses in the arts frills to the curriculum rather than an integral part of it. One reason for this may be, as Yankelovich, Skelly and White report in "An Arts Education Report," that too many see arts classes as "'exposure' to the arts." Perhaps "we should think less of 'exposing' children to the arts and instead focus more on integrating arts and artistic ways of thinking/teaching more completely into school curricula and even their own lives." The delineation of skills presented in Fowler's analysis of the report from the College Entrance Examination Board (pp. 59–60) gives teachers a good beginning for this description of specific learnings in the arts. As these skills and concepts are delineated for individual courses, teachers may also realize additional relationships among all areas of education.

Shortly after I was asked by NEA to edit a book on fine arts education, I visited the Art Institute of Chicago. While viewing George Bellows's "Love in Winter," I thought of the relationship between viewing this painting and considering the role of fine arts in the curriculum.

When I moved very close to the painting, looking at the figures individually, the images became distorted and indistinct. As I stepped back the figures became more distinct and I could see the individual images in perspective. Often, teachers are so close to their own subjects that the courses become distorted; they fall into the trap of examining the individual "lines" of the course at the expense of the overall view. As a curriculum coordinator with systemwide responsibilities, I, too, find that I tend to move too close to a specific curricular area or project under development. When this happens, I have to step back and place the curriculum into proper perspective with the entire educational process. Then, relationships become visible. This collection of essays should be viewed in the same way. While each has meaning by itself, a greater meaning becomes apparent when each is considered as part of a whole. The entire collection examines and exemplifies the role of the fine arts in the curriculum simultaneously.

Notes

[1] *The Humanities in the Schools*, Harold Taylor, editor, Citation Press, New York, New York, 1968. p. 56.

[2] Frederick B. Tuttle, Jr. "We Can Teach Students to Write." *Connecticut English Journal*, Fall 1977. Frederick B. Tuttle, Jr. *Composition: A Media Approach*. Washington, D.C.: National Education Association, 1978.

Chapter 2

EXCELLENCE IN EDUCATION: THE ROLE OF THE ARTS

Arthur D. Efland

The function of the arts in general education is a perennial issue. There have been times when the arts were heralded as remedies for the ills affecting schools and society itself. Now, however, as new crises change educational priorities, the role of the arts is again in question. What role should they play in today's schools, given the rising demand for excellence? Will increased concern for basic education preempt the arts? This article begins with some examples of the arts in the history of schooling in America in preparation for looking at the problems today.

HISTORICAL BACKDROP

The common school emerged in the 1830s and '40s as the first true public school. It purported to provide practical education in all things useful to citizens, for whom the work ethic was the dominant orientation. In this stringent setting the arts put down their first tentative roots, starting with music. For Horace Mann (1841), it was a way

> to improve the hearts, as well as develop the intellects of the pupils. Good feelings, and pure tastes and elevated sentiments, can be nurtured. Already this is done. How has music made our schools radiant with happy faces! Who now doubts its benefits? . . .
> Every pure taste implanted in the youthful mind becomes a barrier to resist the allurements of sensuality. (p. 186)

Music was a kind of moral education, inspiring pupils to do good deeds, despise indolence, and love one's country. Common school educators developed and reinforced values to sustain the social order. Music became an integral part of their strategy to resist the alien values that came with massive immigration in the 1840s.

In the post-Civil War era the schools were asked to respond to the demands of the industrial revolution. American industrialists began to see that their manufactured goods could not compete in international trade with the products of Europe. A group petitioning the Massachusetts legislature wrote:

> Our manufacturers therefore compete under disadvantages with the manufacturers of Europe; for in all the manufacturing countries of Europe free provision is made for instructing workmen in drawing. (Massachusetts Board of Education, 1871, Appendix C, pp. 192-198)

The school had to meet the crisis of industrial competition, and in Massachusetts the solution was drawing instruction.

In the 1930s the nation was struck by the worst single economic catastrophe in its history, the Great Depression. Banks failed, and people lost their life's savings. Alien ideologies like fascism and communism began to look attractive to those who had lost hope. The school once again was the agency of redress and responded by teaching the values of social cohesion. "Art in daily living" and "art in the community" were the themes that were emphasized, for social alienation was the problem of the time, and once again the arts were asked to repair the social fabric.

With the onset of World War II, art classes made posters urging the sale of war bonds; theatre groups put on skits dramatizing the danger of spreading rumors; and choral groups inspired feelings of patriotism and raised morale.

Looking back we see that at one time the arts supported industrial growth; at another, a form of community action; at a third, psychological therapy, and so forth. Throughout the history of education, the changing role of the arts must be understood in terms of the social demands that affected general education.

These changing mandates affected all subjects. In the late '40s when the school was pushed toward a "life-adjustment" curriculum, subjects like algebra and trigonometry were replaced by business math, only to be reintroduced as disciplines in the early '60s. Yet in spite of these changes, the need for mathematics and language was recognized. This was less true for the arts since their role in most industrial societies is ambiguous.

Reprinted with permission from *Theory Into Practice*, Autumn 1984, © 1984 by College of Education, The Ohio State University.

In past societies they were bound up with religion; in the monarchies of Europe they glorified the ruler as the symbol of the state; in Marxist countries they function as propaganda; but thankfully, no set of officially dictated purposes yet governs their use in our society. We know the arts are good but what are they good for?

THE CURRENT STATE OF EDUCATION

In the 1970s we saw a resurgence of emphasis on basic skills. As the time spent on reading, language, and mathematical computation increased, there was a corresponding decline in time spent on social studies, science, and the arts. Now, after more than 10 years of such emphasis, with more than 70 percent of the school day tied to "the basics," the net yield is profound skepticism. Massive expenditures for the development of programs in basic skills and new testing and evaluation techniques have managed to raise a few test scores but they have not allayed the pervasive fear that the quality of education has undergone decline. The report of the National Commission on Excellence in Education concluded that quality has declined to such an alarming extent that we are "a nation at risk" (National Commission on Excellence in Education, 1983).

Some educators, citing taxpayer revolts and inflation, blame the situation on eroding economic support for schools. Others look at the ways the curriculum has become fractured by conflicting demands on the school. Chapman (1982) explains:

This fragmentation of the curriculum has been caused by a general failure of the educational establishment to reconcile two major demands on schools. The first demand is located in the traditional role of the school as an agency for transmitting organized knowledge to each generation. The second demand is found in our expectation that schools will promote the individual and social growth of children by teaching them to be literate, to have self-esteem, to seek jobs, and so on. The first demand is accommodated by the *content* children learn through instruction based in the major subject fields—science, social studies, and the arts. The second demand is met through the *patterns of behavior and skills* which schools attempt to cultivate—skills in reading, in communicating with others, skills that are essential for securing a job, and participating in civic affairs.

When we look at the regular curriculum today, we can see that these two demands are poorly reconciled. What we now see is a curriculum where instructional time for the arts, sciences, and humanities is bartered for time to teach special courses that purport to nurture the individual growth of children— courses that build self-concepts, or teach creativity, skill in critical thinking, perceptual awareness, moral judgment, or other skills. . . . In short, the so-called basic skills are taught with little regard for the content children are learning in social studies, the sciences, or the arts. (p. 16)

EXCELLENCE VERSUS EXPEDIENCE

How do we achieve excellence in schooling? Where is it found? What role can the arts play in its attainment? Is it a national trait to compromise excellence with expedience? The unstated policy of planned obsolescence that has dominated the automobile industry illustrates this practice. Until foreign competition provided an alternative, consumer choice was limited to cars that began to deteriorate within months of leaving the showroom. Rejection on the part of consumers provides a form of marketplace accountability. With the introduction of foreign automobiles American consumers were no longer tolerant of the inferior products they had been receiving from domestic sources. The president's commission on excellence places the blame for this on a willingness to get by with a minimum of effort:

In contrast to the ideal of the Learning Society, however, we find that for too many people education means doing the minimum work necessary for the moment, then coasting through life on what may have been learned in its first quarter (National Commission, 1983, p. 472).

Were people less satisfied with doing the minimum to get by, the problems faced by both industry and the schools would not exist. What the commission report could have added was the idea that doing things well is to make an art of them. *Haute cuisine* is cooking done with superb skill, experience, and knowledge. Well-made machines become works of art; well-designed buildings become architecture; and when schools provide excellent teaching we say it's an art. Anthropologists who have studied the highly artistic people of Bali have noted that there is no word in their language for art. When asked they say, "We have no art—we just make things as well as we can."

In like fashion Logan (in Chapter 8) notes that ordinary movements become dance when they become aesthetic. Art in Dewey's sense of the word is "an experience"—the ordinary made extraordinary. All great art reminds us of the possibility for excellence in human accomplishment. In our own time this is one of their principle functions. To achieve excellence in education we need to make it artistic, by providing the arts to be sure, but also by making teaching an art. We need to attend to the aesthetics of the teaching process, but before we do so we need to see why the curriculum in basic skills has failed. The argument that I advance takes issue with its lack of attention to aesthetics.

SOURCES OF DECLINE

Evidence indicates that during the post-Sputnik era (1957-64) students achieved higher scores in mathematics, computation, and reading than did comparable students before that time. Yet in the years between 1964 and 1978, the academic gains of the previous period were nearly wiped out (*Metropolitan Achievement Test Special Report*, 1971a; 1971b). The decline was greatest among high-school pupils, was less among children in the middle years of schooling, and children at primary levels showed a slight increase in achievement. Changes in educational practices during the '60s and '70s might help explain these effects.

Most significant among these changes were the widespread introduction of "new math"; the adoption of open-classroom methods of instruction; the introduction of systems of individualized instruction such as "mastery learning"; the decline in the use of basal readers for teaching reading; and in 1969, the introduction of the television program *Sesame Street*. The latter may account for the higher levels of reading readiness in the primary grades; the new math for lower computational skills (it was not designed for computation). But why was there a downturn in reading achievement levels beyond the primary grades? The adoption of open-classroom approaches and individualized instruction by systems such as mastery learning are possible causes. Common to both is a reduction of the teacher's autonomy and control.

Typically, mastery learning systems use sequentially organized teaching materials in various subjects and skill areas. Students are to master each packet before proceeding to the next. They progress at their own pace, and on completion of the material, are rewarded with more of the same. "Individualized instruction" is perhaps a misnomer, for only the rate of instruction is controlled by the learner. He or she has no control over the content, nor is there much provision for differences in learning styles. Though in theory the rate at which students learn is determined by aptitude (Carroll, 1963), some researchers suggest that the results might also be influenced by procrastination on the student's part (Yeazell, 1975). If the teaching material carries little intrinsic reward and the only incentive is to be given more of the same, the students may show less inclination to work hard. As early as 1971 Bloom, one of the theoreticians for mastery learning, recognized the problem:

> What the teacher believes to be the rewards which influence students positively may under some conditions have the opposite effect. This research indicates that there may be almost as much variation in the reinforcers that influence students as there is in the aptitudes they possess. Eventually, we must find techniques for appraising the reinforcers for individuals. And, of course, we must find methods of helping teachers learn to use a greater variety of reinforcers as well as relate reinforcers to individual needs. (pp. 38–39)

This is an alarming confession because it admits that one of the major components in the mastery strategy (finding adequate ways to reinforce learning) was inadequately researched. Reinforcers are agents that act as rewards or punishments because they evoke pleasure or pain. They can take the form of praise by the teacher or can be found in the intrinsic features of the instructional materials. If these have sufficient zest or variety to be experienced as pleasurable, there is incentive to continue with the task. But if they become highly routinized or predictable, the learner becomes bored.

This may help explain why achievement test scores declined on a national scale at precisely the time when 3,000 school districts utilized some form of mastery learning. Since these declines were most dramatic at the upper elementary and secondary levels, it may well be that after a few years of such routine, curiosity is stifled.

AESTHETICS, STRESS, AND THE LEARNING PROCESS

To maintain psychological equilibrium in living and working, human beings need to have changes in pace and routine. We seek sensory enrichment, novelty, and surprise not merely for amusement but for our psychological well-being. Going to a better restaurant, traveling, celebrating a holiday, visiting a museum—all these call into play aesthetic stimuli. Were it not for these occasions, life would become dull. Unending routine is not merely dull, it is psychologically stressful, and such stress is debilitating. Is it any less so in the school environment?

It is no coincidence that for thousands of years people have used the arts for psychological stimuli—from the hymn before a sermon to the ritual dance before a battle. Daniel Berlyne (1968), a Canadian psychologist, was interested in explaining why the arts have these properties. He found that in both human beings and higher primates there is a drive to seek "biologically neutral stimulation," i.e., stimulation that is not involved in seeking food or escaping pain but which is pursued for its own sake because it is self-reinforcing. These are encountered in a variety of situations: in the arts, in sport, in children's play. Berlyne also suggests they are probably higher in information content as well. He writes:

> Rises in arousal generally mean increases in "alertness," "attentiveness," "emotionality," or "interest" in what is being perceived at the moment. They are accompanied by an increased readiness to act on the part of the musculature and an increased capacity of the central nervous system to take in and process information about environmental events. (Berlyne, 1968)

If we look for the elements of novelty and surprise in mastery learning, we look in vain. Instead we find predictability and routine. Used to excess, these aspects create stress for the average learner and acute discomfort for bright students. The concept of reward in learning theory and the qualities which make the arts pleasurable suggest that the connection is more than coincidence. Though situations which facilitate learning need not always be pleasurable, the approaches to basic education have been unrelentingly tedious. If the tedium had some demonstrable benefit it might be justified, but the record of accomplishment suggests otherwise.

THE CHALLENGE OF EXCELLENCE AND THE ARTS

The arts were only cursorily mentioned in the National Commission on Excellence in Education's report. Its writers were intent upon the pursuit of excellence in the traditional subject matter fields—language, mathematics, science, and the like. Clearly they have discovered that education in the basic skills, especially as it has been practiced in the last decade, has not produced these abilities, for literacy is more than the ability to read, write, or manipulate mathematical symbols. In Eisner's view it is the ability

> to secure or express meaning through what I shall call *forms of representation*. Literacy may be regarded as the generic process of being able to "decode" or "encode" the content of these forms. Because conception and expression are as diverse as any of the sensory modalities humans can use, literacy can be employed, developed, and refined within any of the forms of representation the sensory systems made possible. (Eisner, 1981)

These forms of representation enable us to conceptualize and express meanings in a variety of ways. To be literate in this expanded sense means being able to use a variety of forms of representation. Eisner notes that schools tend to neglect the development of literacy in many of the forms of representation used within the culture.

The creation of a balanced curriculum is one of the most pressing curriculum problems of the day. Although our understanding of cognition is far from complete, it is becoming apparent that there are differences between thinking with images and with abstract symbols, and that oftentimes they are interconnected. This not only suggests that human understanding is enriched by the use of images, but that their absence in learning may impose limits on the kinds of meanings we can derive from our experience. Human intelligence has various ways of forming thought, some of which involve the kinds of images found in the arts. Yet we structure curriculum and teaching as if the arts do not contribute to our ability to understand.

Although Eisner would expand the definition of literacy to include the forms of representation involved in the arts, it would be a mistake to conclude that these images operate as functional equivalents to verbal forms. In his paper on the structure of knowledge in the arts, Broudy (1966) uses the example of a dance:

> If the dance is a caricature (a sketch) of war, of death, of love, of tragedy, of triumph, our perceiving becomes serious in the sense that we are beholding an expression that is also trying to be a statement about something so important, so close to the big issues of human life, perhaps so dangerous, so revolting that we have not yet formulated a language to state it clearly. (p. 35)

Broudy was describing the power of art to evoke feelings and ideas, but he also noted that the arts express meanings that are not accessible in other symbolic forms.

A CURRICULUM FOR EDUCATIONAL EXCELLENCE

If educational excellence is to become a national goal it will require more than minimum competency in basic skills. Changes in curriculum are needed which once again place the domains of knowledge at the center. Chapman (1982) describes a curriculum consisting of three broad areas of content: the arts, the sciences, and the humanities. The arts would be subdivided into literary, performing, and visual arts; the sciences would be grouped into physical, biological, and earth sciences; and the humanities would include history, philosophy, and the social studies. Language and mathematics as basic skills would be encountered in the primary grades as subjects in their own right and in all the other subjects as well.

> A curriculum built around these studies in these three areas is probably the single most well-established standard for quality in the education for youth. It is the kind of education valued by persons who occupy positions of leadership and power in our society. While this standard has not been seriously entertained for public schools in recent history, it might well be revitalized as the issue of quality continues to be linked with the very survival of public schools. A curriculum designed for excellence need not be for the wealthy alone, nor based on the assumption that all students will attend college. (Chapman, 1982, p. 15)

While Chapman's proposal may sound radical, it is supported by the fact that in school districts where the arts excel, other academic studies are generally in good repair. The arts are rarely singled out of red-carpet treatment and are often the last areas to receive adequate economic and moral support. Thus when they are found to be strong, it is likely that the total program has quality as well. Conversely, if strength in the arts is lacking, other parts of the program are probably wanting, for the quality of the arts is a barometer that serves to indicate the levels of economic support for the total school program.

SUMMARY AND DISCUSSION

The arts have played a number of roles in education: support for industry, moral education, social cohesion, and therapy. Given the problems facing education today, this article posed the question "Do the arts have yet another remedy to offer a public school system plagued by academic decline?" As a prelude to answering this question I attempted to answer the prior question, "Why have we witnessed this period of decline?"

My analysis focused on the inability of present methods, in particular mastery learning, to provide adequate reinforcement of learning because of a lack of a sense of novelty, complexity, and surprise—qualities which psychologists tell us are found in the arts. These qualities do not merely add to one's sense of pleasure in learning; their omission from the instructional situation produces stress and boredom which can be psychologically debilitating. To be sure this is a technical argument. I did not delve into the social reasons why the curricular reforms of the '60s, which began to show beneficial results in most areas except mathematical computation, were abandoned. Why did professional educators forsake this direction in favor of a return to the basics? Was it the rising cost of education? Was it a concern over educational equality? Perhaps the historians of education will tell us at some future date.

A second analysis of the problems of education cited Eisner in arguing that the arts use forms of representation through which meanings may be understood that cannot be apprehended with ordinary verbal or mathematical symbols. His argument expands the conception of literacy to embrace the ability to encode and decode meaning from a wider array of symbol systems including those provided by the arts.

But in order that schools might achieve literacy in this more comprehensive way they will need to redress the balance within the curriculum itself so that it deals with more than verbal and mathematical symbols. The outline of such a curriculum is suggested by Chapman who describes three main branches: the arts, the sciences, and the humanities. Chapman notes that wherever educational excellence abounds, especially in the schools that serve the more privileged elites in this country, these three features are invariably present. Why should it be any less so for the rest of society?

To the question, "Do the arts offer a remedy to the problems of education today," the answer is no. *The arts have no new remedies to offer.* The remedy will be found in a broad conception of general education where the arts, the sciences, and the humanities are each adequately represented. Only when these are all part of general education will there be excellence in education.

References

Berlyne, D. (1968, July). *The Psychology of Aesthetic Behavior.* Paper presented at Pennsylvania State University.

Bloom, B. (1971). "Mastery Learning and Its Implications for Curriculum Development." In E. Eisner (Ed.), *Confronting Curricular Reform.* Berkeley, CA: McCutcheon.

Broudy, H. (1966). "The Structure of Knowledge in the Arts." In R. A. Smith (Ed.), *Aesthetics and Criticism in Art Education* (pp. 23–45). Chicago: Rand McNally.

Carroll, J. B. (1963). "A Model of School Learning." *Teachers College Record, 64,* 723–733.

Chapman, L. (1982). *Instant Art, Instant Culture: The Unspoken Policy for American Schools.* New York: Teachers College Press.

Eisner, E. (1981, March). "Mind as Cultural Achievement." (Dewey Memorial Lecture). *Educational Leadership, 31,* 466–471.

Mann, H. (1841). *Common School Journal, 3.*

Massachusetts Board of Education. (1871). *Thirty-Fourth Annual Report: 1870.* Boston: Author.

Metropolitan Achievement Test Special Report, 1970 Edition (no. 15). (1971a). Equivalent scores for metropolitan achievement tests, 1958 edition, in terms of metropolitan 1958 model-age grade equivalent. New York: Harcourt Brace Jovanovich.

Metropolitan Achievement Test Special Report, 1970 Edition (no. 16). (1971b). Equivalent scores for metropolitan achievement tests, 1970 edition, and Stanford Achievement Test, 1964 grade equivalent. New York: Harcourt Brace Jovanovich.

National Commission on Excellence in Education. (1983, July). *A Nation At Risk,* reprinted in *Communications of the ACM, 26* (7).

Yeazell, M. (1975). "Self Pacing and Procrastintion in Mastery Learning." *Educational Research and Methods, 8* (1), 5–8.

Chapter 3

ADDRESSING THE ISSUES: THE CASE FOR THE ARTS

Charles B. Fowler

The need to sustain and improve the arts in education is, perhaps, more critical today than ever before. Public and political concern about the quality of public schools continues to escalate. Numerous new educational studies and reports point up serious deficiencies in the American educational system. Pressures for improvement and change are mounting.

Taken by themselves, these are positive signs of the public's genuine interest in matters educational and their growing willingness to give priority to the solution of educational problems. But set in the context of a decade of curtailments of arts education programs across the country, failed community school bond/tax proposals, the widespread public press for accountability, the pervasive influence of test scores and college entrance requirements, and the seeming momentum and appeal of the back-to-basics movement, arts programs could face further cuts or the threat of them. Competency-based testing, accountability, and proscribed curricula, often popular with state legislators, are too often the mechanics of those who would cut out the "frills" and develop a bare-bones curriculum.

American education does, indeed, suffer from a host of very real problems, but sophomoric and simplistic solutions will not suffice. Further curtailments of arts programs are not the answer. To make certain of this, those who understand the arts and believe in their educational potential and worth must be ready to come to their defense.

In the national, state, and local debates on education that are certain to be generated by recent and forthcoming educational studies, policies governing the arts in education will be reevaluated and reconstituted. Support for the arts in education will be crucial to these discussions, to the reassessments, and to the drafting of new educational policies.

If the arts are to establish their stature as an educational basic, a convincing case must be made for their real value in the education of every citizen. And that case must be laid before the American people and the educational powers-that-be. As Thomas A. Hatfield, art consultant with the South Carolina Department of Education, has stated: "The problem is not to work harder at what we are already doing, but working smarter within the political matrix of schools."[1] We must build our case with care.

A COMMON CAUSE

It is equally important that we build our case *together*. At a recent conference on "The Future of Musical Education in America" held at the Eastman School of Music in Rochester, New York, Russell P. Getz, president of the Music Educators National Conference, pointed out that one of the root problems is factional bickering and the splintering of the profession—what Robert Freeman, director of the Eastman School, later referred to as music's insular "islands." That theme was further reiterated by Charles Leonhard, professor of music education at the University of Illinois, who spoke of "the divisiveness and competition that divide us." In this regard, Leonhard called for a "common cause for the arts."

If the splintering into islands is a characteristic within each art field, it is a problem between the arts as well. Hatfield reminds us that parity begins at home:

Arts educators have been so concerned about promulgating the values and concerns of our own conditions, so involved in protecting our feudal rights as freemen, that we have consequently segregated ourselves from our colleagues. We really have no peer group in the functional sense of the term. Because each of us (art, music, drama, dance) has developed separate monologues we have not truly profited from each other. It is interesting to note that when administrators, curriculum coordinators, and the public view major portions of school programs, science and social studies are simply referred to as the science or social studies program—not astronomy, biology, physics, geography, or history. The arts are not viewed in such umbrella terms, and as such, are not viewed as major components of the school curriculum. The art room here, the music room over there, or a drama class down there—these are appendages.[2]

Reprinted with permission from *Arts in Education / Education in Arts: Entering Dialogue of the 80's*, National Endowment for the Arts in Education, 1984.

In building a case for the arts, fragmentation can cripple. Two truisms come to mind: The left hand must know what the right hand is doing. Two hands are better than one.

THE NATURE OF OUR CLAIMS

Agreement may not come easily. For many years arts educators have based their arguments about the role and value of the arts in education on two basic—sometimes conflicting—philosophical viewpoints. The first is a utilitarian philosophy—that the arts are to be valued because of their practical or instrumental contributions to human development. The second derives from aesthetic philosophy—that the arts have their own intrinsic qualities that make them worthy of inclusion in the education of every person.

We tend to expend a great deal of effort disagreeing with each other over our claims for the arts. Assuming the aesthetic view, Vincent Lanier, professor of art education at the University of Oregon, says:

> What emerges from a review of art education theory during the last 40 years or so is a desperate and constantly changing attempt to legitimize the teaching of art on instrumental grounds. We do not insist on the educational value of art because its proper role in our lives is a significant end in itself, but because we believe that through art we can promote other outside-of-art behavioral developments.[3]

Contrast this statement with the thought of Thomas Barone, assistant professor of education at Northern Kentucky University, who suggests that "it is an overreliance on the 'art-for-art's sake' arguments that has, regardless of their intrinsic solidity, partially contributed to the sadly consistent relegation of the arts to the curricular caboose."[4]

But there are strong advocates for the aesthetic justification of arts education. In discussing a substantiation for arts education set forth by Edmund Burke Feldman, president of the National Art Education Association, Ralph A. Smith, editor of *The Journal of Aesthetic Education*, says that Burke's rationale favors the instrumental side and fails to indicate "that art is something to be enjoyed, that the experience of art is a supreme sort of delight or human gratification."[5]

Music educators, like their art education counterparts, have just as much difficulty agreeing on their basic rationales for music education. In an issue of the *Music Educators Journal* devoted to this subject, Gerard L. Knieter, professor of music and dean of the College of Fine and Applied Arts at the University of Akron, opposes claims based upon instrumental values. He says: "They support the study of music for nonaesthetic (nonmusical) reasons. Any profession that seeks justification apart from its subject is on shaky ground."[6]

In the same issue, Patricia Coates, adjunct assistant professor of music at Georgia State University in Atlanta, states that "one of the tenets of aesthetic theory is that music is valued for its purposelessness. A facet of the curriculum that believes in its own lack of utility is doomed."[7]

Kenneth H. Phillips, a doctoral candidate in music education at Kent State University, poses two provocative questions: "Must it be utilitarian versus aesthetic? Or can our philosophy embrace both?"[8]

Yet we must make this case, as Jacques Barzun implores us, without inflating the rightful claims of the arts to special merit. Such inflated notions, he says, expand the "plausible or possible into the miraculous." The danger of inflating ideas, he reasons, is that "you cripple your teaching, for the ideas misdirect it. And you deceive your students by false promises raising false hopes."[9] Boards of education, the public, principals, superintendents, and teachers will usually see through inflated claims and react accordingly.

Rationales for the arts carry implications for teaching. In choosing a rationale, we infer the content (curriculum) and methodologies of the arts. Every "why" means "what" and "how." But what one claims for the arts must be deliverable. Practice must match rhetoric. All rationales must be evaluated in the light of this simple rubric.

Notes

[1] Thomas A. Hatfield, "Arts, Politics, and Change in the Schools," *Arts Education and Back to Basics* (Reston, Virginia: National Art Education Association, 1979), p. 193.

[2] *Ibid.*, p. 188.

[3] Vincent Lanier, "Enhancing the Aesthetic Potential," *Arts Education and Back to Basics* (Reston, Virginia: National Art Education Association, 1979), p. 101.

[4] Thomas Barone, "Things of Use and Things of Beauty: The Swain County High School Arts Program," in *Daedalus: The Arts and Humanities in America's Schools*, Vol. 112, No. 3 (Summer 1983), p. 25.

[5] Ralph A. Smith, "Professor Feldman and the NAEA Take AIM: An Agenda for Further Discussion," *Art Education*, Vol. 35, No. 5 (September 1982), p. 18.

[6] Gerard L. Knieter, "Aesthetics for Art's Sake," *Music Educators Journal*, Vol. 69, No. 7 (March 1983), p. 35.

[7] Patricia Coates, "Alternatives to the Aesthetic Rationale for Music Education," *ibid.*, p. 31.

[8] Kenneth H. Phillips, "Utilitarian vs. Aesthetic," *ibid.*, p. 30.

[9] Jacques Barzun, "Art and Educational Inflation," in *Art in Basic Education*, Occasional Paper 25 (Washington, D.C.: Council for Basic Education, 1979), pp. 6 and 7.

Chapter 4

AN ARTS EDUCATION REPORT: GROUP DISCUSSIONS WITH TEACHERS

Yankelovich, Skelly and White, Inc.

This is a report on a series of discussions with teachers from public elementary and secondary schools that were finalists for, or winners of Rockefeller Brothers Fund Awards in Arts Education. The report examines top arts teachers': (1) personal characteristics and goals; (2) views about teaching today; and (3) views about the ingredients of successful teaching.

This study suggests several interesting findings.

- These top arts teachers appear relatively similar in most respects to what one might expect to find among top performers in other professions;

- Teaching the arts can be an isolating experience—most top arts teachers view society's understanding of the value of arts education as lacking;

- At the same time, the arts provide teachers with a multitude of good teaching modes—these teachers have clearly grasped these opportunities.

  — They are also employing a variety of tools to cope with the isolation inherent in their job.

Probably the single conclusion these discussions point to most clearly is that much needs to be done to help society better understand the integral role that the arts can play in educating young people.

WHY THIS INQUIRY

In any profession one of the regularly posed questions is what distinguishes successful practitioners from others. In August, 1984, a Seminar of Exploration with a group singled out by the Rockefeller Brothers Fund Awards in Arts Educations program provided an opportunity to explore that question with a number of successful music, dance, drama, visual art, and creative writing teachers. This memorandum summarizes a number of observations based on discussion sessions held with these successful arts teachers.

By way of background, the Seminar of Exploration involved about 30 outstanding arts teachers in a 5-day conference. The Seminar was sponsored by the Ahmanson Foundation, the National Endowment for the Arts, and the Rockefeller Brothers Fund, with the assistance of the Massachusetts Higher Education Assistance Corporation. The goals of the seminar, and its multi purpose agenda, are described in a seminar overview available from the Fund. The Observations in this report are based on a series of four two-hour focus group discussions, each with eight or nine of the recipients, during the seminar.

The discussions were moderated by two Yankelovich, Skelly and White professionals, David Richardson and Patricia Sze, who led each discussion using a loose discussion outline as a guide.

Two caveats are in order. First, these observations can only begin to tap some of the personal views and characteristics that make these individuals unique. Second, a strictly scientific data gathering procedure would also include individuals who have *not* displayed any particular signs of excellence for comparative purposes. That is beyond the scope of this inquiry. The focus in this document is on noting similarities and dissimilarities *among* this group of outstanding teachers.

Observations address three sets of questions:

1. Who are these individuals: Personal background, personality, relation of teaching and art to their lives, personal goals?
2. How do these people view teaching today? Are they optimistic? Pessimistic? Do they get satisfaction from it?
3. What are the ingredients of successful teaching? How do they approach teaching? Who/what helps or hurts?

Who Are These People

Recognizing that these individuals are primarily representative of themselves, it is interesting to note some

Reprinted with permission. © 1985 by the Rockefeller Brothers Fund.

personal characteristics. These 30 people cover the spectrum of arts disciplines—visual arts teachers are most widely represented, but some teach music, drama, dance and creative writing. About half teach in elementary or secondary schools, while the remainder teach in high schools. They are both men and women, tend to be over 35 years old but most are under 50, most are married and have children. This profile suggests they are not dramatically different in these respects from what one would expect to find among professionals from other fields in the prime years of their careers.

Demographic Profile of Seminar Participants

	Elem./Jr. High School Teachers	High School Teachers
Sex	⅔ women	⅔ men
Age	30–45	35–49
Marital Status	⅔ married	Almost all married
Kids	Half have children	⅔ have children
Parents	Very diverse	

Attitudinally, these top arts teachers also resemble top performers in other fields. They are strongly self-confident, have a huge level of satisfaction with what they are doing now, exude energy, and express a strong desire to continue the learning process. They are also balancing different roles; most split relatively evenly in describing themselves as artists/teachers. High school teachers are slightly more likely than others to place the balance more heavily on artists.

Of all professions, teaching is probably the one that children have the most opportunity to observe as they mature. The impact of this is reflected in the number of teachers who relate their decision to teach back to their own student days. Many of these teachers came to the profession because of a particular mentor, or a teacher they had at some point in their own student career. Interestingly, that influential person was as frequently someone they came into contact with at a very young age as at an older age such as in college.

Looking to the future, most of these teachers appear to have made a continuing commitment to teaching. As with any such group, some are seriously questioning their own future involvement in teaching, though most are not. However, virtually all are grappling with the balance between teaching and their art. In this regard, most appear to want better feedback on what/how they are doing.

Though discussed surprisingly little, the issue of compensation clearly is a big concern. The concern stems from doubts about whether, in the future, good people will want to get involved in teaching the arts. While it is certainly an issue, compensation does not appear to be the primary concern shaping these teachers' views about their careers.

Teaching the Arts Today

While there is considerable diversity of opinion among these arts teachers about the state of the profession today, one major theme that clearly runs through most conversation is the view that society at large has a woefully inadequate understanding of the purposes and value of arts education. The extent to which this perspective is stated exceeds that which one might expect to find in any profession that simply has a specialized purpose. Perhaps this is a reflection of the general scrutiny the education system is being exposed to today, though several discussion themes suggest it is more than that. This perspective is clarified somewhat by several sub-themes.

- Asked what barriers exist to children doing arts today, the vast majority of comments focus on societal expectations; a view of the arts as frivolous, or a frill; misperceptions about the role of talent, what it takes to be good and what it means.
  - Weak school support systems and fear of failure on the part of students follow behind as barriers to children doing more arts.
  - Fear of failure could very well be a derivative effect of society's misperceptions about the arts.

- Many of these arts teachers indicate a view that most potential support groups too often have an insufficient understanding of the role the arts can play in education.
  - One of the most lucid answers to this issue came in response to a question about whether children get enough "exposure" to the arts. One arts teacher characterized this view of the arts as part of the problem—suggesting we should think less of "exposing" children to the arts and instead focus more on integrating arts and artistic ways of thinking/teaching more completely into school curricula and even their own lives.
  - Despite considerable diversity in individual situations, these arts teachers label their principals as the single most important and potentially most supportive aid to them. Other teachers outside the arts are rated surprisingly low in the level of support they typically provide.

- There is *not* agreement among these arts teachers about the future prospects for the field.
  - Considerable hope for the future is mixed with, in some cases, extreme pessimism about the impact of back-to-basics approaches to schooling.
  - Overall, however, there is not a sense that the tide of public opinion is moving overwhelmingly against the arts.

These views about where the arts fit in school programs lead top arts teachers to a strong self-directed orientation. One of the strongest themes to emerge from these discussions is the view that teaching the arts permits great freedom, but is often accompanied by a sense of isolation. The freedom comes from the opportunities for creative use of alternative teaching approaches—tapping the multiple intelligences that Howard Gardner, a Harvard psychologist, speaks about in his book *Frames of Mind: The Theory of Multiple Intelligences* (Basic Books, 1983). These arts teachers frequently comment on this contrast with other teachers, and the few who teach both arts and other subjects talk about the internal conflict created from the limitations of the other disciplines. Some even venture that this greater scope of teaching vehicles is why teaching the arts is more fun. Most importantly, these teachers appear to be using this freedom to take initiative in the teaching of the arts.

The freedom is almost inherent to teaching the arts. The isolation is not, and the strength of feelings of isolation vary substantially from individual to individual. Is the sense of isolation debilitating? Perhaps for some, but most of these individuals appear to cope either through internal strength, by being in a unique institution that provides strong support, or by building a base of support that begins with students and grows outward.

Internal strength is an intangible. Teaching the arts appears to provide individuals with a stronger sense of personal identity than is the case with other teachers, by virtue of their recognized role as artists. This appears to be the case particularly with high school arts teachers, for whom their identity as artists is as strong or stronger than their identity as teachers. This, coupled with the broader teaching opportunities mentioned above, forms the basis on which individuals can develop their personal coping mechanisms.

Institutional support is also relatively good for these top teachers. While a number have situations where the school administration is neutral, unclear about their role, or less than ideally helpful, virtually none are shackled with an administration so restrictive that it impedes the individual's ability to work.

One of the more frequently-mentioned coping strategies is the building of a grass-roots base of support. In a sense this is a substitute for top-down influence such as that discussed frequently now in math and sciences. A number of these teachers are mobilizing their students, and often parents or the broader community, to advocate for the arts. Teachers of the arts have a unique opportunity to reach out in this manner because, by their nature, the products of arts education are meant for display.

Virtually all of these top teachers cope using at least one of these mechanisms; several have clearly developed each.

INGREDIENTS OF SUCCESSFUL TEACHING

In light of their views about teaching the arts, it is not particularly surprising that top arts teachers place the greatest emphasis on their own personal ability to stimulate students. The chart [that follows] illustrates the approximate impact these arts teachers believe five key components have on successful teaching (recognizing that this quantifies an essentially qualitative concept).

RELATIVE CONTRIBUTION OF 5 COMPONENTS TO GOOD ARTS TEACHING

PEERS (9%)
SCHOOL ENVIRONMENT (14%)
KIDS (18%)
CURRICULUM (21%)
YOU (38%)

Several points stand out.

- Virtually all of these top teachers resist the idea that *any* children are not teachable, or that the arts are not appropriate for them.
  - A sub-theme here is resistance to the idea that children need to reach any particular level of proficiency in the arts.
  - A striking point made very frequently is that the arts allow the teaching of personal life skills to at least the same extent as they serve to convey specific arts skills. In fact, many of these teachers define this as their primary teaching function.
- These teachers rely very heavily on themselves, and surprisingly little on peers.
  - And they rate their own charisma, or personal enthusiasm, as the key factor in their success, to a greater degree even than their arts skills.
  - Asked to describe their greatest personal attributes, these teachers cite in order: their talent or knowledge, their dedication or commitment, energy, enthusiasm, imagination, humor and clarity in communicating.
  - Emphasis is placed on the teacher's role as translator, using the variety of teaching methods at their disposal to help students learn.
- The most important environmental factor in the eyes of these teachers is a relatively general concept, characterized variously as a spirit of mutual support, ownership, warmth, community.
  - Exposure to the arts (product) is seen as the most direct way of creating this sense.
  - In descending order, teachers also rate as important time (for the program and for themselves), money for resources, and comparable pay.

— There are many differences in assessments of these environmental forces.

GOALS AND CHALLENGES

These discussions point to a number of conclusions about appropriate strategies for the future. The two big challenges relate primarily to arts teaching as a profession:

1. Arts teachers need to help translate for society at large an understanding of the proper role that the arts can and should play in teaching.

2. And more specifically, the case for integrating the arts into school curricula and into people's life-styles needs to be made more convincing.

Several strategies suggest themselves for addressing those needs:

3. Gardner's multiple intelligence concept is a powerful and convincing notion that could go a long way toward helping people understand the fuller value of arts education.

4. One area where there appears to be continuing confusion is measurement of success—how to do it, what should it be, and how should success measures be used.

5. Like groups everywhere, arts teachers can take a lesson from politicians and marketers by more thoroughly understanding who their constituents are (and using this knowledge to mobilize support in the most effective way): Who cares what they do? Who can help? Who can hurt?

Finally, at the personal level, the single question most in need of answer is a common one; how do you strike a balance between different personal role patterns?

6. One strategy that could offer answers to both personal and professional questions is already being pursued to some extent by many of these top teachers: go to the community, to build support for an arts program and to gain personal sustenance and compensation.

Chapter 5

WHAT ARE CHILDREN DOING WHEN THEY CREATE?

Robert Alexander

This world is not of a child's making. Very little in the world has to do with children's immediate point of view. When children create, they are making sense of the world they see, hear, smell, touch, taste, feel (emotionally), and think about.

The moment of creation is probably the only time children's culture is validated. It is an expression of who children are way, way down in the most important part of themselves. It is a time when children do not have to worry or fret about being accepted. Children can be who they want to be *fully*. *The child is in control of the moment*. They do not have to ask anyone how they should express their point of view. When children are deeply involved in and concentrating on the discipline of creation at the moment of creating, they *are* communicating their point of view. There are few, if any, opportunities for children to express their point of view in our society's normal environments.

The human animal is a thinking, learning and creating organism. Children who are creating are using themselves fully. All of their senses are fully operating at one hundred percent optimum capacity. Children's emotional, intuitive, intellectual, conceptual, and physical apparatus is fully involved. In the moment of creation, children are making and remaking the world in their hopeful, hateful, anguished,joyous, and wondrous images.

At birth, we are each in a highly developed state of creative genius. The natural behavior of the human animal is to create, to allow the unconscious to bring into being shapes, sounds, forms, and colors of flowers, trees, mountains. . .the fantastic symphony that is life.

As children create, their imaginations are alive, vibrant and fully operative. Their fear of the unknown vanishes. Children are seriously and joyously embarking on a journey of exploration and discovery. They are captain and pilot of the vessel.

The imagination is like a muscle. It must be used constantly if it is to retain the brilliance of its ability to transform and focus. Rousseau said that the world of the imagination is a limitless one. As children journey amid the creative splendor of the mind-heart-soul, their imaginations are constantly opening new doors and windows, showing new avenues of approach and hinting at mysteries which lie beyond what they can see. The imagination is keeping the brain so deliciously alive that its potential is achieved. Only in the creative act is the brain's potential achieved. The brain is constantly expanding. Thoughts and feelings are experienced with magnificent clarity, crystal sharpness and control. All of life's bewildering chaos is transformed into harmony and truth.

In the act of creation, children are closer to their truth than at any other time. Children can fully express their humanistic feelings of caring deeply about other people, about nature, about animals, about *life*.

Children's involvement in the artistic creation at a time in life when their verbal skills have not yet fully developed allows their *full, articulate expression* of who they are and what they feel, think, and want to have happen and want to be.

Inherent in any work of art are problems to be solved and the process of wrestling with the solving of those problems expands children's growth effectively and cognitively. In the artistic act, the right hemisphere of the brain is stimulated, a stimulation that does not occur during children's usual daily functioning at home or in school.

When children are in a creative state, their powers of concentration and conceptualization from reality to the abstract, from the abstract to reality, from the symbolic to the literal, and from the common to the symbolic, are constantly and increasingly being nurtured and expanded. High levels of consciousness—what Abraham Maslow calls peak experiences—occur within children during the act of creation.

In the act of creation children are truly *free*.

Reprinted with permission from *PTA Today*, March 1985.

Chapter 6

ART, CREATIVITY, AND THE QUALITY OF EDUCATION

Jon J. Murray

Several years ago, a student approached me with a college recommendation form and a question: Was it appropriate, she wondered, for me to recommend her for admission to this school? She pointed to the instructions at the top of the form, asking her to have it filled out by a "teacher who has taught you an *academic* subject in the last two years."[1] The word stood out like a serious warning, and I remember having second thoughts about accepting the form—because I am a teacher of art.

In secondary education—and in its narrowest sense—"academic" refers to the subjects of English, foreign language, history, economics, mathematics, and science. But in a broader sense, it pertains to the "liberal arts, or to the realm of ideas or abstractions."[2] As I continued to read, I became convinced that this prestigious Eastern university wanted to hear from me as much as from anyone else. "Please comment on the nature and quality of the applicant's academic work," their second request read. "Evidence of strong motivation, creativity, and the ability to work independently is especially helpful."

If these three qualities are the most pertinent characteristics of academic work, then there is no high-school subject more academic than art. No one is pressuring high-school students to study art; rather, serious college-bound students are especially urged to take other subjects instead. Thus, when they do pursue the arts, it is evidence of "strong motivation." Furthermore, "the ability to work independently" is an obvious prerequisite for artistic activity. Although students at work in the art classroom can and do evaluate one another's work, and offer constructive criticism, making an original work of art is for the most part a risky, lonely affair; students are expected to invent their own solutions, often to problems that are also of their own invention. And it is common knowledge that "creativity"—the deepest, broadest, most complex kind of thinking—is uniquely emphasized in many American art programs.

Nevertheless, the degree to which the art-making process is misunderstood by parents, school administra-

tors, and teachers of other subjects is a constant source of surprise to most teachers of art. Art-making is neither the mechanistic application of skills and techniques nor the passive representation of visual sensations. Nor is it—as it must often seem to those who have never tried it—the mindless flow of some innate, mysterious, inspirational juice. Like other forms of expression, art is a language, a context for interpreting experiences and constructing meanings. It is the visible manifestation of thought.

CREATIVITY

All children make art, and what looks like spontaneous play is also the serious business of learning about the world—learning to perceive, to distinguish, to organize, to form concepts, to express, to understand. Art teaches us to see actively, to see into and to structure what we see, to think with our eyes. A human being, unlike a camera, cannot look at something without thinking about it. If we consider how many of our "vision" words are also our "thought" words—insight, viewpoint, imagine, study, reflect—we will understand that perception cannot be separated from cognition.

"All knowledge has its origin in our perceptions," Leonardo told us, and Cézanne knew this when he said, "Nature is on the inside." All artists and scientists realize that what we know depends on what we see; and what we see depends on *how* we see. Art inquires into the "how" of seeing. A work of art gives us, above all, a way of seeing, and at the same time, a way of knowing and of caring.

Like the writer expressing ideas by arranging words in meaningful combinations, so the artist gives form to thought by manipulating line and color into new, expressive relationships.

This manipulation of verbal or visual symbols into patterns involves a complex series of decisions. I tell my students that drawing is like playing a game of chess. All chess games begin with the pieces arranged in the same way, and all drawings begin as blank pieces of pa-

Reprinted with permission from Daedalus, *Journal of the American Academy of Arts and Sciences* (The Arts and Humanities in America's Schools) Summer 1983, vol. 112, no. 3, Cambridge, MA.

per. But each chess game, each drawing, proceeds differently, because a different set of choices is made. The player/artist makes a move, evaluates the resulting situation, makes another move, and so on. The changing circumstances require constant reevaluation, and future moves must be planned, strategies developed, previous knowledge tapped, and risks taken. The chess player must try to imagine all fruitful possibilities that fall within the boundaries of the rules—but the artist must go further. He or she must go beyond the "rules" to the very edge of what is conceivable and what is possible, must push to extend this edge, to press beyond previous boundaries, to break the rules, to deepen and widen the scope of the "game," and to fit another piece of the unknown into the expanding realm of the understood. This is true intellectual growth. The goal in art is not to play a "good game" or to make another "pretty picture," but to challenge the old formula, to reinvent or improve the "game" itself through the adventurous use of all available mental and visual faculties.

Going beyond lesser forms of intelligence, this daringly expansive kind of thinking and learning that we call "creativity" requires intuitive sensing; imaginative positing; playful manipulation; waiting, watching, and being open to the unexpected; allowing and taking advantage of "happy accidents"; coping with risk, confusion, and anxiety; and being able to relinquish old patterns in order to synthesize the new, the better, the more meaningful. The creative process itself is

> a long series of leaps of the imagination and the artist's attempts to give them form by shaping the material accordingly, . . . a strange and risky business in which the maker never quite knows what he is making until he has actually made it. . . . No wonder the artist's way of working is so resistant to any set rules, while the craftsman's encourages standardization and regularity.[3]

The creative attitude is a questioning one; it thrives on independence, heightened sensitivity, the pleasure of direct experience, and the thrill of achieving something original. Institutionalized education, while giving frequent lip service to the importance of creativity, usually stands firmly on the side of "standardization and regularity" instead. By favoring the predictable, the efficient, the practical, and the measurable, schools inhibit the capacity for spontaneous invention, for fantasy. When Einstein said, "The gift of fantasy has meant more to me than my talent for absorbing positive knowledge," he underscored the importance of rediscovering the creative potential that our practical, rational institutions often smother.

ABSTRACTION AND ANALYSIS

Everyone can develop more creative ways of thinking. As a high-school art teacher, my task is not to tell my students *how* to see, but to help them discover the ability to see in their own individual ways. Many people use their eyes for not much more than identifying and measuring. To come in out of the rain, I must identify the door and gauge its distance and direction; to read, I must identify words and phrases by their shapes. Art teaches students to see actively, to think and feel with their eyes, to grasp the visual and aesthetic qualities of what they see. Active seeing is analogous to active reading, where critical, thoughtful reading means not merely understanding the plot, but grasping fully what is meant.

Most students will "read" a painting only for "plot"; once they determine what it represents—what it is a picture of—they look no further. In a museum, they spend more time reading the labels than looking at the art. They are mystified by abstract pieces—angered, even, by what they cannot comprehend—and reassured by representational works with descriptive titles. They look to identify, but not to understand.

Robert Motherwell once pointed out that of the subjects taught in school, mathematics and music are more abstract than art. Yet, most adolescents have no trouble working with mathematical symbols and find nothing especially puzzling about a sound that has no lyrics. Why, then, are abstract paintings so bewildering? Why, for example, is geometrical abstraction more acceptable in a math textbook than in an art gallery? Unfortunately, this is largely a matter of conditioning. But there is at least one other reason people feel comfortable with representational art: it has the capacity to imitate the appearance of visible reality. It is a constant marvel to many how the flat surface of a painting can seem like an opening into deep light-filled space, how a figure, meticulously sculpted, can almost be caught drawing a breath. Writers often attempt to match the descriptive power of visual art. Joseph Conrad seemed to say this when he wrote: "My task which I am trying to achieve is by the power of the written word, to make you hear, to make you feel—it is, before all, to make you see."[4]

Adolescence, nonetheless, is an important time to develop the ability to think abstractly, to consider abstract concepts and qualities apart from particular, concrete situations. In art class, as in English class, students learn to manipulate and express abstract ideas by working with them firsthand. They come to recognize the abstract qualities of all art, and learn that if they do not understand the paintings of Piet Mondrian, they will not really understand those of Jan Vermeer.

With good high-school art instruction, students can learn to see much more than likeness, just as with good literary instruction, they can learn to read much more than plot. They learn how to analyze the structure of a work and to see how this structure contributes to its meaning. They separate the work into its parts—sentences or lines, paragraphs or shapes, sounds or colors—and they figure out how these parts relate to one another to form a coherent, significant whole. By analyzing Shakespeare and Michelangelo, students learn how to admire and appreciate; but by analyzing their own works, they learn how to grow.

EVALUATION

Art instruction has a significant advantage over other disciplines in this regard because students, by working side-by-side and seeing what others are doing and thinking, have the opportunity to analyze, criticize, and evaluate each other's work. As they observe someone else's approach to the same problem, or to a different one, they can react immediately. They question each other, reinforce each other, make suggestions, and share insights. In some educational settings, this is called "cheating." In an art class, it is students helping each other to learn through constructive criticism based on mutual respect. A weakness found in a work, far from pointing to a weakness in the student, is an insight, a revelation, a gift—a clue that points toward future growth and direction. In art, students spontaneously seek and offer criticism. In art, there is no profit in knowing something the next person does not, no need to conceal the answers from another.

"Evaluation" involves making judgments based on internal evidence and by the application of external standards; it is a vital part of the creative process. Each time a line is drawn or a form is altered, the artist steps back to evaluate this change in the context of all previous decisions, by grasping the work as a whole. The separate, concrete, nonlinear, visible presence of artwork facilitates this grasping, this "stepping back to think about your thinking." One of the most difficult judgments to make is that the work is finished, that the idea has emerged in its best, most final form. The tools are set down, but the evaluation continues: outlines of the next piece are already taking shape in the mind.

In a high-school art class, students constantly evaluate their own works-in-progress; they share informal judgments about each other's unfinished works; they evaluate "finished" pieces in formal class critiques; they receive ongoing criticism from the teacher; and they reevaluate their previous works again and again in light of recent discoveries. We would find an equivalent situation in a creative writing class where students share their rough drafts with one another; read and discuss revised works as a group; receive formal criticism from the teacher in front of (and for the benefit of) everyone else; and continuously reevaluate the growth of their own ability to write.

At Mamaroneck High School where I teach, artworks judged by the art department to be of particular quality are frequently displayed in the high-school gallery. They then receive further evaluation from a much wider audience of peers, other teachers, administrators, parents, and the general public. This wider recognition provides a powerful incentive for student artists. It creates a stronger sense of community, and it allows the department to establish and maintain higher standards of excellence.

How do art teachers grade their students? How can the effectiveness or quality of a work of art be judged? Artists, art educators, and art critics have no trouble dealing with this question, although they may disagree on which criteria to stress. But those untutored in art often have great difficulty with these judgments. They admire works that "look more real," that "seem more attractive," or that show them something familiar. Abstract art seems arbitrary, standardless, devoid of skill and content. Art is seen as a "do-your-own-thing" activity with no definite criteria of evaluation. Beginning art students, incidentally, often try to cover their weaknesses with this myth; they may attempt to justify inconsistency, oversight, or sloppiness in their work by saying, "But I meant it to be that way!"

There is, of course, more than one effective way to approach an open-ended problem, and this principle is basic to the creative problem-solving process. This does not mean that "anything goes" or that there are no solid standards for evaluation. Evaluating a sculpture or an essay is certainly more complex than correcting a fill-in-the-blank test. The latter is simply a case of right or wrong: Did the student recall the appropriate bit of information or not? The former requires analysis of a series of intelligent decisions, carefully woven into a coherent, meaningful composition. An essay reveals not only what the student is thinking, but how well he or she is thinking, and how well he or she can write. Similarly, a work of art—whatever the specific content—also shows the depth and quality of the student's thinking, and his or her command of the visual language. The work in both cases can be evaluated in two ways: on the basis of content—the quality, depth, and originality of the ideas expressed; and on the basis of form—the clarity and effectiveness of the organizational structure, and the level of craftsmanship in the execution.

Paintings, like dreams and poems, must be approached with a fresh eye and an open mind. Prejudice and presumption must be held in check, and the picture must first be evaluated on its own terms, on the basis of internal evidence. For if a picture is a vision, a "way of seeing," we must let it show us how it is to be seen.

What is happening in this picture? What immediate, overall tone or feeling is conveyed? What do I notice about it first? How does my eye travel through this field of visual elements and forces? Is there an overall structure that I grasp? What parts do I distinguish? Are they similar or different? In what ways? Do similar parts reappear? How are they arranged? Do they form patterns? How are they related to each other? How do they function? Do all the elements carry equal emphasis or weight? Why or why not? How do the parts relate to the whole? What kinds of decisions were made? What sort of "game" is being played? Do all the elements and forces achieve some kind of balance and coherence? Is there anything within this context that is haphazard or out of place? Is there anything that seems purposeless, unnecessary, contradictory? What interests me the most about what I am seeing?

A picture sets up its own rules—its own internal grammar and logic—and it succeeds or fails according to those rules. Each picture is an attempt to expand the artist's vocabulary, to create new and better ways of using the visual language. However "accidental" some aspect of a picture may seem, the decision to leave it in must be seen and judged as a conscious and deliberate one; if it is not included on purpose, it has no business being there at all.

In addition to evaluating the work on its own terms, the art teacher will consider it in the context of the student's previous achievements and in light of the goals of the assignment. Although art problems never have one correct answer, they often have different degrees of open-endedness. Like writing problems, many are designed to strengthen specific skills and techniques for using the language. The final product can thus be evaluated objectively, as evidence of the level of mastery of the particular skills in question.

Narrowly defined problems have another important use: they invite comparison of the solutions. Students are constantly surprised at the range of possible responses to the same problem. They are able to judge relative degrees of originality and levels of craftsmanship, and discover differences that do not imply "better" or "worse." These are the subjective aspects of the work that reveal personality characteristics, individual preferences, and the uniqueness of each artist's "handwriting." The importance of enjoying these subject qualities of the work cannot be overemphasized; the resulting "awareness-of-self" and "appreciation-of-others" proves that individualized instruction happens best in a group.

As for evaluating each student's work in the context of his or her previous development, the art teacher must judge whether the work reflects the student's current levels of understanding and ability, whether the student has challenged himself or herself to go beyond the specific objectives of the assignment, what new territory has been conquered, and how much growth can be seen. In some disciplines, "initiative" is the mark of a superior student; in art, it is simply expected of everyone. It is the only way to ensure the maximum growth of each student.

Every so often, a student will develop a good formula for making "successful" drawings, and will crank out one impressive piece after another, to the great delight of family and friends. The student has reached a certain level of accomplishment and is resting on a plateau. The formula becomes a habit, a comfortable rut. At this point, the art teacher must challenge the student to go further, to stretch the formula until it breaks, and to begin building a better one.

In teaching art, or anything else, for that matter, the temptation is to focus on the production of "successful results." Teachers who want their students to succeed sometimes make success too easy to achieve, devising problems that can *only* turn out well, requiring students *only* to imitate or memorize, perhaps even "reviewing" the answers before the test is given. In art, the teacher may tell a student what to do in a given situation; even worse, he or she may actually touch a student's work to correct or improve something.

Although many students like to have the teacher do the work for them, others want only advice and the opportunity to make their own discoveries. The teacher can help a frustrated student clarify the problem and envision some of the options, but leave responsibility for the final decision up to the student. Learning to take risks and cope with frustration is an important part of original, creative thinking in any field; in art, it is *central* to good instruction. The teacher must relinquish control over the ultimate success of the work and become an understanding guide, a source of encouragement, criticism, and support.

Good high-school art instruction teaches students to work independently, to assume increasingly greater responsibility for the direction of their own learning, and to develop the skill of critical self-evaluation—to get art students to "act" like artists.

The true importance of evaluation, then, is in teaching students how to evaluate their own work. They must ask themselves: How original was my idea? Did I struggle to develop and perfect it? How well did I organize the elements of my design to achieve balance, interest, and clarity of expression? How efficiently did I use my time? How carefully did I shape my materials? Did I strive for the best execution, or opt for easier alternatives? What level of craftsmanship did I achieve? What are the strengths and weaknesses of my work? How can I improve it? What shall I do next? What have I learned?

When college recommendation forms inquire about a student's intellectual qualities, their questions always specify the importance of curiosity, initiative, originality, self-direction, creativity, and the capacity to think and act independently. These qualities are nurtured more in art than in any other subject area. In art class, more students spend more active learning time doing more different kinds of thinking: intuiting, imagining, recalling, interpreting, reasoning, abstracting, analyzing, organizing, applying, relating, synthesizing, expressing, and evaluating. More than any other activity, art challenges the whole student—intellectually, emotionally, and physically—to learn by doing.

MOTIVATION, CARING, WORK

The other important question on college recommendation forms concerns the student's emotional and personality characteristics: "What are your impressions of this student's character, aims and values? . . . What are the first few words which come to your mind to describe this student's personality?"[5]

In some high-school courses, teachers learn comparatively little about the personalities of their students. In course work that traces a predetermined curricular path, students reveal little more about their emotional makeup and degrees of punctuality, courtesy, talkativeness, neatness, and obedience. When teachers do learn about a student's character, it is often in spite of, rather than because of, the content of the course work. But in art class, students are expected to communicate personal thoughts, feelings, and values through the work itself.

Art is a kind of selection process based on personal values; it "isolates the poetic experience from the accidents and irrelevancies of everyday existence."[6] Making a work of art about something is a way of investing time and effort in it, a way of saying, "This is important. I care about it."

Art-as-caring has powerful implications. Art demands painstaking craftsmanship, and it is this concern that motivates the mastering of skills that in turn increase one's ability to think with and through the material. Craftsmanship demands self-discipline and perseverance, the willingness to supply whatever amounts of time and energy are necessary to ensure the quality of the work.

One day not long ago a student showed me a drawing and asked, "Is this good enough?" Before I could reply, another student jumped in and expressed my sentiments perfectly by proclaiming that "good enough" isn't good enough! We cheat our students when we expect less from them than their absolute best. But by openly caring about the quality of each individual student's art, the teacher fosters a healthy attitude about "work."

Unfortunately, most students think of work as something that you have to do, something that you do in order to get done. Work means answering the teacher's questions, doing the textbook's problems, covering the material, getting the grades, piling up the credits, getting out. High school becomes so much "busy work," something you have to do if you want to go to college. Academic passivity sets in, and school feels more like a place where something is done *to* you than a place for active doing. External pressures and rewards substitute for intrinsic motivation, and learning resembles a food that is consumed only for the sake of survival, not savored for the pleasure that it provides. Thus do we attempt to educate "intellectual gourmets" on a diet of "cafeteria food."

Colleges are well aware of this problem; a question on Brown University's recommendation form is particularly enlightening:

> What do you know of this student's intellectual qualities? We are especially interested in any evidence you can give about the nature of his or her motivation for academic work—the breadth and depth of intellectual interests—the originality, independence, and sensitivity he or she displays in course work—the quality of performance as compared to that of classmates. . . . Is this student self-directed or driven by pressures from family or for status? Is this student studying for his or her own satisfaction or for grades? Does this student approach work creatively or routinely? Does this student pursue studies beyond assignments or does he or she have to be nursed or prodded?

This one paragraph contains more insight into the "mediocrity problem" besetting contemporary American education than many recent lengthy studies. It also points toward the negative effects of most college admissions criteria that emphasize grades and scores while minimizing the nature of a student's motivation.

It is difficult for students to derive much pride and satisfaction from their work when it is not really their work. Determining the same answers to the same problems as everyone else, grasping and rephrasing the teacher's ideas, and "covering material" from the same book discourage self-direction and independent thinking. Even class discussions are often lectures-in-disguise—with teachers leading, hinting, and cajoling their own ideas out of the mouths of their students. Students know when the teacher already has the answer to the question he or she is asking. Instead of thinking about the question, they will often just try to guess what the teacher has in mind. Students are very good at this game; the person who blurts out the most answers the fastest often has the best chance of guessing the correct one.

The "Guess-what-*I'm*-thinking" style of teaching implies that "I'm-not-really-interested-in-what-*you're*-thinking." The experience of creating artwork is in direct opposition to this secondhand, superficial kind of learning. Art provides a context in which students think their own thoughts, make their own discoveries, and experience the satisfaction of true personal accomplishment. Originality means ownership, and pride of ownership is the key to self-motivation. Art students can say, "This is my work; I made it. These thoughts are mine, not the textbook's, and not the teacher's. The feelings expressed here belong to me. I didn't memorize this concept, I discovered it! I created this character, this symbol, this vision. It's different from everyone else's. It's mine. It's me. And it's important enough to be a work of art."

The meaning of art-as-caring expands to art-as-caring-about-my-own ideas. Education is given back to the students, pride of ownership replaces apathy, and students develop a healthy feeling of self-esteem. Faith in oneself—the feeling of being capable—is a crucial precondition for creative activity.

Educational ownership, by requiring students to accept personal responsibility for the nature and quality of their work, can eradicate indifference. When a student complains that the work is boring, I sometimes say, "You're absolutely right; what you've done is boring. Why don't you stop boring yourself and think of something interesting?" Unlike most television shows, my purpose is not to entertain. I am there to challenge my students to excite themselves and to interest each other through their work.

There is often a lot of talk in educational circles

about how to "make learning exciting." As victims of our own system, we are so accustomed to schoolwork being secondhand, routine, and irrelevant that we've forgotten our own role in making it that way. We use the excuse that if something is enjoyable, it can't be work; if it isn't drudgery, it can't be important. This myth is sometimes used to question the significance of art education altogether. But by taking art courses—despite the pressure not to—by frequently working beyond course requirements, and by actively seeking criticism from more than one art teacher, our students remind us of the satisfaction in true creative learning. They work not for the course, the teacher, the grade, or the credit but for themselves and each other—to understand, to make sense of and give meaning to, to care, to share. They make discoveries about everything, but especially about themselves. They are becoming adults by establishing a conscious identity, partly through the creation of "work" that is, above all, their own.

By taking college recommendation forms at face value, one might conclude that colleges must be keenly interested in the creative accomplishments of their applicants, and must, therefore, hold artistic achievement in the highest regard. Yet just the opposite is true. Some colleges give separate consideration to "special talents" an applicant may have; some regard achievement in art to be a "nice extra" so long as the "important" grades and scores are up to par; some even go so far as to cross art courses off an applicant's transcript and then reaverage the remaining grades.

Since colleges almost never require the completion of an art course for admission, high schools—which usually see their main function as preparing students for college—seldom encourage students to pursue the arts. As they progress through elementary, middle, and high school, students are taught that art becomes increasingly less important. When the time comes to think about putting together a transcript that will impress colleges, a second verbal language, upper level math and science, and "AP anything" emerge as major priorities—along with any course in which a student feels capable of getting a very high grade. Making room in their schedules for art becomes a kind of sacrifice for college-bound students, and learning for its own sake inevitably falls by the wayside.

This situation is further complicated by the myth that success in art depends on innate talent. Students who feel that they cannot draw or that they are uncreative often steer away from art to avoid the risk of a low grade.

It is difficult to reconcile this contradiction between what high schools say about creativity and what they do about it. Why are the arts—where creativity finds its greatest emphasis—still discouraged? Why are art programs still the second-class citizens of the curriculum? Why are they among the first to be crippled or cut? Why are they academically suspect? If fine art has been one of the "liberal arts" since the Renaissance, why are so many of our educational institutions still living in the

dark ages? Why this gap between pretense and practice?

One reason seems to be a simple, self-perpetuating lack of knowledge about art. The students of yesterday, who were taught that art is unimportant, are the educational leaders of today. School administrators receive little or no training in art. Visual illiteracy and the consequent undervaluing of the arts is thus passed along in institutionalized form.

Another factor is the current dominance of statistical concerns in education. In an attempt to compare candidates more objectively and efficiently, colleges have come to depend increasingly on standardized test scores. But by trying to quantify learning, we end up limiting ourselves only to what is quantifiable, and the significance of the resulting scores has become a matter of great controversy. What seems apparent, however, is that colleges attach far more weight to standardized test scores than is justifiable, and that this emphasis has a variety of negative effects on secondary education.

To standardize means "to make uniform, to cause to be without variations or irregularities." When we standardize learning, it becomes something that is "neither very good nor very bad"—the definition of mediocrity itself.[7] Colleges complain about the routine, mechanistic, superficial thinking of their applicants; but they have not really faced up to their own role in fostering what a colleague of mine calls the multiple-choice mentality. "In manipulating symbols so as to recite well, to get and give correct answers, to follow prescribed formulae of analysis," Dewey wrote, "the pupil's attitude becomes mechanical rather than thoughtful; verbal memorizing is substituted for inquiry into the meaning of things."[8] Creative art celebrates originality, uniqueness, and open-ended inquiry. It rebels against standardization, regularity, depersonalization, mediocrity, and adherence to prescribed formulas. It encourages deep and divergent kinds of thinking that defy easy quantification.

By depending on standardized test scores and grade-point averages, colleges must somehow then make meaningful distinctions between applicants. This seems to be the function of recommendation forms: "Most helpful are specific examples of the applicant's academic commitment and talent and personal qualities or accomplishments that make this person unique. We depend on your evaluation to help us distinguish among our many qualified applicants."[9] It is ironic that colleges claim to value examples of a student's uniqueness and originality, while virtually dismissing the firsthand evidence of creative achievement in art.

FUTURE DIRECTIONS

What should be done? There has been much discussion recently about a dangerous decline in the quality of public school education. Many simplistic solutions have been proposed, including more math, more science, more homework, more hours in the school day, and more school days in the year. More of the same will only produce more of the same, unless steps are taken simultaneously to improve educational quality.

Art programs can make a critical contribution to this improvement if they do not fall victim to budget cuts, misguided reforms, myopic college admissions policies, and federal leadership in the wrong direction. The kind of creative thinking and self-motivation generated by good high-school art instruction can be used as a proven model for other disciplines—and for secondary education in general.

First, art should be elevated to a position of complete parity with other academic subjects. This parity should be reflected in a school's philosophy, as well as in its graduation requirements. Expenditures for art staff, work space, and materials should be comparable to similar expenditures for science programs. Graduate degree programs for school administrators should reflect the importance of art in the curriculum; and high-school principals should learn exactly what to expect from (and how to support) a quality art program.

Second, college admissions policies should give the same weight to art courses that they give to other academic courses, less weight to standardized test scores, and much greater weight to genuine creative achievement in *all* subjects. Judging creative ability in art presents no real problem. Several organizations, including the Advanced Placement Program of the College Board, have developed effective models for doing this; art schools do it routinely. By properly evaluating portfolios, colleges can get a unique, firsthand look at the quality of their applicants' work: the depth of their thinking; the power of their logic and imagination; the development of their skills; the range of their concerns; and the time, care, and energy that they invest in what they do. Colleges can help improve secondary education dramatically by demanding such solid evidence of creative accomplishment. They can also help themselves to a good look at what an applicant *can* do, instead of relying on test scores that tell more about what an applicant *cannot* do.

Third, art should be used as a model for other subjects in an effort to increase active learning time, creative problem-solving skills, critical self-evaluation, motivation, and meaningful social interaction between different kinds of students. Let me provide an example.

One day I discovered a student of mine memorizing biology notes for an upcoming test. I wondered out loud why art and science are taught so differently, since art-making and science-making are essentially the same process. Both, after all, are attempts to investigate and better understand the world by using observation, creative experimentation, and study to produce results. The class reacted violently to this assertion; everyone knew there just *had* to be a huge difference between art and science, but no one could say what it was. Finally, one student explained that science is "facts," while art is "whatever you feel."

Behind this response lurk two unfortunate misconceptions: that science is a closed system of unchanging actualities, neatly recorded and waiting to be memorized; and that art is a collection of arbitrary doodles, sometimes beautiful but always inconsequential. Since these misconceptions result from the way art and science are frequently regarded by schools, I asked my class to imagine a science course taught the way art is usually taught, and an art course taught the way science is usually taught. As a painting teacher, I would use a textbook that presented contemporary painting as an established body of knowledge. As a biology teacher, I would show my students how to use a microscope and then send them down to the pond to see what they could discover.

One student objected, saying that in order to do science, you first need to learn a great deal of background material, and that a high-school student at a pond with a microscope would not be able to discover something that is not already known by scientists. I ended the discussion by asking the students if, in their artwork, they had discovered something that is not already known by artists.

High-school art students are not really making "fine art"; their works will not end up in museums or influence the course of art history. But they do have the important sense that they are making their own discoveries through their work. By acting very much like artists, they come to understand the nature of creative activity. They experience the frustrations, risks, and joys of the art-making process.

By the same token, if my hypothetical biology students figured out their own way of classifying a small portion of the animal kingdom, they would learn firsthand the challenges and thrills of making science. For the same reason, math students should act more like creative mathematicians, history students should act more like historians, and English students should act more like authors.

There is no lack of educational literature about the living death caused by fragmented, compartmentalized rote learning. Accumulating knowledge is important, but it is certainly not enough. According to Sidney J. Parnes,

Without knowledge, there obviously can be no creativity. By way of analogy, we might consider the kaleidoscope, wherein the more pieces we have in the drum the more possible patterns we can produce. Likewise, the greater our knowledge the more patterns, combinations, or ideas we can achieve. However, merely having the knowledge, the bits and pieces in the kaleidoscope, does not guarantee the formulation of new patterns. One must "revolve the drum," manipulate the knowledge by combining and rearranging the facts into new patterns. In the mind, these new patterns are ideas. . . . Without imaginative manipulation, abundant knowledge cannot help us live in a world of change. And without the ability to synthesize, evaluate, and develop our ideas, we achieve no effective creativity.[10]

The three reforms I have suggested constitute a significant step toward the achievement of "effective creativity" in our schools. This step will not be inexpensive, but it will accomplish much more than the qualitative improvement of secondary education. In addition to preparing better college students, it will help all students to prepare for a better life.

The business community has warned us of the shrinking need for unskilled labor, the dawn of the "information age," and the importance of imaginative problem-solving in a rapidly changing world of high technology. Only by developing creativity—our greatest natural resource—can we hope to prepare students for jobs that do not yet exist. Of greater importance, however, is the need for creative solutions to the unprecedented social, political, and moral problems that jeopardize the future itself.

Our goal is not to make every student an artist, but to exploit art as a unique vehicle for developing the individual creative potential in every student. As an open-ended, unrestricted context for thinking and caring, art expands our capacity to perceive, understand, and appreciate life. Limited only by the power of our imaginations, art confronts the unknown and attempts the impossible in order to construct new meanings. Art exalts the best and the most that human beings can be; it inspires us to surpass ourselves.

Students who work for creative satisfaction more than grades and credits will become adults who value wisdom more than wealth and status. They will not confuse "making a life" with merely "making a living." They will be leaders, not just survivors, because they will see living as an art—and art as a way of living.

Artwork is thus a metaphor for lifework in its fullest sense. In art class, students learn that a good work of art has interest, balance, and wholeness; that it seeks clarity and simplicity for the sake of truth. Good artwork is shaped with sensitive caring as well as courageous imagination. It radiates self-potency and a sense of purpose. It is a creative adventure and an ongoing act of love. Should a good life be anything less?

Notes

[1] Yale College Teacher's Recommendation for Applicant (New Haven: Yale College Office of Undergraduate Admissions, 1982).

[2] *Dictionary of Education, Third Edition*, edited by Carter V. Good (New York: McGraw-Hill, 1973), p. 3.

[3] H. W. Janson, *History of Art*, 2d ed. (New York: Harry N. Abrams, 1977), p. 11.

[4] William Sparke and Clark McKowen, *Montage: Investigations in Language* (London: Macmillan, 1970), p. 224.

[5] Brown Confidential Teacher's Reference (Providence: Admission Office—The College, Brown University, 1982).

[6] I. A. Richards, *Principles of Literary Criticism* (New York: Harcourt, Brace and World, 1928), p. 145.

[7] *Webster's New World Dictionary of the American Language* (New York and Cleveland: World Publishing, 1970).

[8] John Dewey, "The Abuse of Linguistic Methods in Education," in *How We Think* (Boston: D.C. Heath, 1933), p. 238.

[9] Cornell University Letter of Reference (Ithaca: Office of Admissions, Cornell University, 1982).

[10] Sidney, P. Parnes, "Creativity Development," *Handbook on Contemporary Education* (New York: Bowker, 1976), p. 498.

Chapter 7

DRAMA IN EDUCATION: A CURRICULUM DILEMMA

Michael O'Hara

Drama in education, the literature suggests, is founded on notions of the education of the emotions, imaginative insight, the role of creative expression in education, and the affective development of the child. Possibly because of its intangible aims and as yet unarticulated developmental processes, its application within the classroom has not achieved widespread acceptance. Not surprisingly, drama is marked by diversity of practice, with those involved in the area appearing "unable or unwilling to speak for themselves with authority and unity in both academic and practical terms" (Norman, 1971). This article explores the role of drama in education and focuses on aspects contributing to its problematic curriculum standing.

THE DEVELOPMENT OF DRAMA IN EDUCATION

Although drama activities have been included in curricula for many years, Clegg (1973) suggests that drama teaching has not advanced conceptually since Caldwell Cook's pioneering work at Perse School, Cambridge, around the turn of the century. Such a view is disputed by those who recognize Slade's (1954), Courtney's (1968), and Way's (1967) substantial contributions to thinking about the role of drama in education. What is not given serious consideration, however, is the likelihood, implicit in Clegg's position, that the process model of drama in education which has evolved through the intervention of people like Slade has provoked the curriculum issues now surrounding the field. Some discussion of the contribution of these "pioneers" may help clarify the issue.

Cook (1917), in the spirit of Rousseau and perhaps John Dewey, advocated dramatic method and dramatic activities for their inherent value of approaching texts through allowing pupils to develop an empathy with characters, mood, situation, and content, "by doing and from experiencing." Implied in his emphasis on drama activities was a belief that a reflective set must be built into education, "a theory which Britton [Britton & Scott (1970)] and Burton (1955) developed so ably in their respective fields of English and drama" (Scott, 1975). Although Cook's work seems to have been geared toward the creation of drama "products," the use of dramatic method in curriculum practices which he advocated was not immediately built on, and "although many speak today of the 'Play-Way,' few follow his excellent practice" (Hodgson & Banham, 1972).

In the early '40s, drama based activities began to be seen as developmental processes with the work of Laban (1960) in creative movement and A. L. Stone (1949) in movement and mime. Laban's treatise "The Mastery of Movement" recognized that movement education was essential in both the artistic and psycho-social development of all human beings, and Landy (1975) reports that Laban's work formed the rationale of the curriculum of Stone's Primary School in Birmingham, England, where all lessons were taught "the movement way."

The dramatic activity used by Stone, however, was not the playmaking approach adopted by Cook, but was, as Landy (1975) suggests, creative dramatic movement as advocated by Laban. Thus, while Cook had recognized the value of dramatic improvisational work in the teaching of texts, Stone, influenced by Laban, was advocating dramatic activity as an open-ended, exploratory, developmental process in the child's sense. Although the curriculum practices in Stone's school were presented to a wider audience in *Story of a School* (Stone, 1949), there is not evidence available that Stone's curriculum had any real effect on dramatic curriculum practices in English schools at the time.

Peter Slade (1954) is recognized as being the first to attempt developing a rationale for drama in education as a creative subject in its own right. His basic argument was that child drama is an art form, and that drama processes being with the "spontaneous, egocentric creations of the child in sound and movement and [develop] into the spontaneous creation of play, produced and acted by children" (Slade, 1954). This concept of children's development through drama, although largely based on his own empirical observations, evolved to become the "holy writ" and the curriculum crutch of those seeking an autonomous identity for the drama teaching field.

Reprinted with permission from *Theory Into Practice*, Autumn 1984. © 1984 by the College of Education, The Ohio State University.

Attempts, however, to define a separate curriculum identity for drama were at least partly responsible for dulling the debate and clouding the earlier attempts to see drama as being a learning process and having a central role in the English curriculum. But in the mid-'60s, while creative drama continued to attempt to define an identity of its own outside the English teaching field, English was developing a new tradition based on a "personal growth model" (Dixon, 1967), which had much in common with many of the "rough-hewn" philosophies and pedagogies of the drama fraternity.

While there is no dispute about the value of drama to the English teacher, Dixon (1967) argues that the relationship between drama and English has more to it than the borrowing of certain teaching techniques. Drama in the English curriculum continues Dixon, implies a view of education that is child centered, and which accepts the need for the emotions to be educated with the same sense of purpose and responsibility as the intellect. More is involved than providing texts for study or analysis, suggests Creber (1965). Rather, the medium must be harnessed to a continuous process of self-discovery which, he points out, is a particular concern of the English teacher.

Advocates of the "growth through English" paradigm of English teaching in the late '60s and '70s endorsed a central role for drama as a creative medium contributing to self-expression, language development, and "textual" study. Barnes (1968) recommends, in fact, that not only should drama activities be a part of all English teaching, but that all English teaching should approach the aspirations of drama teaching with greater emphasis on "experiencing" and less on academic studies of literature and language. However, the roles outlined for drama in the English curriculum should not, many believe, be seen as a justification for subsuming drama in an overall concept of English teaching.

Slade's articulation of drama's separate curriculum role was advanced to some extent by Courtney's (1968) attempt at conceptualizing the field by exploring the interdisciplinary nature of the subject with perspectives for its ideology wrung from educational thought and practices. Way (1967), on the other hand, considered child drama in a practical context for teachers. "Start from where you are" was his advice to practitioners anxious to use drama in the classroom, basing his approach on a humanistic vision of the child and seeing drama as a practice for living through which children are permitted opportunities to develop their full potentialities. Way also saw drama in education as having a dual function in the curriculum, both as "a method as well as an art," but he insisted that drama could only be seen as a tool for teaching other subjects when it existed in the curriculum as a subject in its own right.

Through the influence of Slade (1954), Courtney (1968), and Way (1967), drama in education developed in its English context as a developmental, creative process and was thus steered away from the production of dramatic artifacts, a movement associated with drama educa-tion practice in the United States—built supposedly on notions of rational curriculum planning. Due, however, to the "rough-hewn" nature of the processes advocated by its pioneers, the field lent itself to highly individual perceptions of the methodologies to be employed in achieving the humanistic and developmental aims of the area. Thus the '60s produced an abundance of texts on drama teaching and prompted Payne (1976) to declare that the decade saw a proliferation of drama teaching texts more noticeable for quantity than quality.

Pick (1967), in an attempt to make a detached appraisal of conflicting views, flung a sobering thought into the drama teaching area by suggesting that the drama teaching fraternity "will have little effect, and will probably do their subject no good by claiming that it is more than they know it is, or by claiming results of which society will approve." Drama teachers can do no more, he insisted, than help children to reexamine some of their own motives for acting as they do. There can be no other branch of teaching, Pick continued, in which the practices of the working artist are felt to be so completely different from the practices of the educator.

Here was at least an implied suggestion that clarification of the role of drama in education as a creative process may best be found through tracing more systematically the links between drama and theatre. Allen (1975) follows this line of thought by posing the question, What are the basic elements in drama through which emotion is expressed? Are we right, he asks, in relying as ever on situation, character, language, and movement? If this is the case, he claims, then these are the traditional elements, Aristotle's demands. The difficulty in defining the role of drama in education, Allen concludes, is that we continually separate drama from the theatre arts.

The delineation of the role of drama in education may well clarify the issues which at present reverberate throughout this teaching field. But Allen (1955) himself 20 years before wrote that the difficulty in even writing on the subject of drama in education is the "problem of describing techniques which are themselves difficult to define in language that has not been fashioned for that end." It is doubtful whether such a parsimonious language for describing the contribution of drama in the development of the child has evolved as yet. However, much writing in the field has attempted to clarify fundamental issues relating to its role, in an effort to rationalize the mythology of terms with which drama teachers surround themselves, and which to a large extent are indefensible (Clegg, 1973).

The Arts and the Adolescent Project[1] was probably the first major attempt to approach this rationalization, fueled by a conviction that the mythology of terms and ad hoc curriculum practices common to all arts areas were symptomatic of a general malaise across the whole of the arts curriculum. A brief examination of curriculum concerns in creative arts teaching and an attempt to place drama in education in the context of the creative arts may cast some perspectives on this possibility.

THE CREATIVE ARTS AND THE CURRICULUM

Since the educational scene began to take cognizance of the role of creative expression in education, the arts have moved from a skills base toward the promotion of children's creative expression through the various arts areas. But Ross (1972) reported that teachers of creative arts experience great difficulty in producing statements of aims for their subjects, and many teachers question the validity of such an exercise at all.

In fact it would appear that once aims and objectives have been formulated, the same teachers recognize how easily their course statements can appear suspect when subjected to traditional yardsticks of curriculum planning. They are usually extremely general and on occasion purport to be the panacea for all curriculum ills by being in the service of the "full development of the individual." Arts teachers, claims Ross, are in need of a curriculum structure and framework upon which they can display their methodologies and content, not only for viewing by a skeptical layperson, but also as a neutral, objective framework which might make tangible their convictions about the creative role of their areas and the intuitive nature of their teaching.

While perhaps accepting that many arts teachers are involved in a search for curriculum respectability, it is important that the basic premises upon which they build their work are explored and taken into account before prescriptions are made. Although teachers of creative arts are inclined to base their educational ideologies on humanistic and phenomenological perspectives of the education process, they would appear to be in agreement in pointing to the crucial role of creative expression in children's development. From this base, the creative arts see their role in the education of emotions through the provision of processes for the exploration of experience, feeling, and emotion.

Creative arts teachers, however, while generally subscribing to creative expression as the broad banner philosophy under which they operate, are beginning to realize that highly individual translations of this philosophy into the different arts subjects are unlikely to stand up to close curriculum scrutiny. But it is not the educational value of particular arts subjects which is the pressing issue, even though there is some movement within arts areas to clarify individual subject identity as a strategy for curriculum respectability. Of more importance is the larger goal of defining the general role of the arts in education, because it would appear that it is only through a clarification of this larger issue that individual arts areas will find their curriculum niche.

There is obviously no overnight answer to this problem, but nevertheless many commentators believe that an answer must be sought out and energies applied to the search. Ross (1972) suggests it will no longer be sufficient for arts teachers to protest that an explanation for their work "is all as impossible as explaining the smell of leaves," because while one can understand what they mean in an intangible sort of way, arts teachers are being pressed not simply to offer explanations for other people, but also to find ways of understanding which can be of use to themselves in the curriculum.

The problematic nature of arts education, as exposed by the *Schools Council Enquiry I* (1968), prompted the setting up of the Arts and the Adolescent Project. The study was completed in four years and the resulting text, *The Intelligence of Feeling* (Witkin, 1974), offered arts teachers a conceptual framework which might form the basis for curriculum development in the arts. Certainly Witkin's attempt at conceptualizing what he identifies as the phases of the creative process was an important impetus to the arts in education debate, but Pythian (1975) worries about Witkin's lack of suggestions for specific curriculum materials, "preferring a generally theoretical solution which will disappoint teachers in search of more practical advice."

Although the Arts and Adolescent Project recommendations have not as yet been allowed sufficient time for empirical testing in the classroom, Ross (quoted by Clarke, 1977) at the Schools Council and Arts in Education Workshop (June 1977) speaks of "a sense of researchers having failed to deliver." For many people present at the workshop, reports Clarke, this was clearly the case. The function of creative arts teaching in the classroom still presents something of a curriculum dilemma and will probably continue to do so until arts teachers put to the test "the received bases of their activities, and endeavour to present a new, clearly argued rationale" (Clarke, 1977).

All of these general issues are clearly preliminary to the specific issues of drama in education. The mapping from general to specific will not be simple, exact, and linear, but we can try to see the problems for drama, at least to begin with, as being partially congruent to those more general problems already discussed.

DRAMA IN EDUCATION AS A CREATIVE ARTS AREA

Clearly the two important issues, that is, (a) the need for planning arising out of modern demand for a form of rationality, and (b) the inherent qualities of the arts subjects seen in their essence to be antithetical to such analysis, are no closer than they were. Implied values in arts education, however, appear to be related to concerns with children's individual growth and "the discovery in each of his or her own personal powers, and the development of confidence in creative ability at whatever level" (Jordan, 1967). The Schools Council Drama Project[2] team reported that drama teachers interviewed in the course of their research revealed a "common concern for the development of the child as an individual" and they further expressed a "commitment to developing powers of imagination through creative activity" (McGregor, 1976).

Allen (1975), in locating drama in education within creative arts teaching, asserts that in all arts subjects the importance of artistic creation is not solely in the making of artifacts but is also the "key process of articulating a complete activity." Subscribing further to Langer's (1953) definition that "the arts are the creation of forms symbolic of human feeling," Allen (1975) states that, in drama, form as the embodiment of feeling is also "the very process by which the creative impulses of children are released and given coherence."

In considering drama in education, however, one must keep in mind that the central activity of the medium is "acting-out," which Robinson (1975) defines as the exploration of ideas, feelings, and impulses in which there is an important interaction between the inner and outer world of the child. The old dichotomy between intellect and emotion can only be overcome, he says, "once it [is] understood that what we know affects how we feel and that perception is inclusive of emotion."

While England (1976) sees the drama teacher's function as that of tapping emotion for educational use with the goal of imaginative insight, Allen (1975) warns that the learnings involved through drama and the arts relate to learning how "to order and control our emotions, and helping them towards an appropriate and creative form of expression." Perspectives on the notion of creative form and control of the expressive media have since been gained from Witkin (1974).

Drama in education, drawing as it does on movement, mime, and role play activities, seems to draw together many of the processes of self-expression. It is, in Rugg and Shumaker's (1928) terms, "the most completely personal, individualistic and intimate, as well as the most highly socialized art. It is rich in content, varied in means, and it represents also an effective union of intellect and emotion." The creative enterprise that we call drama, Wilks (1973) believes, can only be properly defined as an aesthetic event.

Drama in education can be seen to reflect aspects of more general curriculum issues across the arts teaching field. Yet while debates about ideological and epistemological concerns common to all arts areas continue in isolated bursts in the literature, the subjects comprising the arts curriculum pursue their individual search for identity clarification, using their particular aspirations as guides toward the development of curricula and methodologies. A major difficulty, however, is that many of the articulated functions of arts subjects are described in highly abstruse terms, and it is perhaps little wonder that confusion seems to be the hallmark of most attempts to design the arts curriculum.

THE FUNCTIONS OF DRAMA IN EDUCATION

Bearing in mind that the drama teaching area is marked by claims which are unrealistic in terms of curriculum action and design, and heeding Pick's (1967) warning to drama teachers that they must be mindful not to claim that their subject is more than they know it is, an attempt might now usefully be made to identify the functions of drama about which there appears to be some measure of agreement. The identification of the ac-

cepted core assumptions about this area's curriculum role leads to the judgment that it is principally and crucially a learning medium.

In her foreword to *Education Survey 2: Drama* (1967), Lee writes that it is "now widely recognized that drama has a vital contribution to make in education." The nature of the contribution, she continues, is "to self discovery, personal and emotional development and to the understanding of human relationships." The *Primary Education in Scotland Report* (1965) sharpens and focuses this view and points to the fact that it is the making of drama, or the participation in dramatic exploration, that has most to contribute to the development of the child. Basic to an understanding of the notion of the making of drama, notes Allen (1975), is:

> an awareness of the area as being concerned with problem solving activity in the context of peer interaction, with a concern to help children articulate their feelings, sensibilities, apprehension and awareness, and in articulating them, embodying them in dramatic form.

Drama is a group, creative activity built on the personal experiences of its participants (Brossell, 1975), and not only reinforces the "known" but could be seen as a way of "finding out about the unknown" (Jennings, 1973).

Davies (1975) sees the medium as a refining of experience, a reliving and reappraisal of experience out of which comes a "degree of self-awareness." The dramatic mode of representation involved in this process combines "all the elements which characterize human behaviour" (Stephenson & Vincent, 1975). These elements, write Stephenson and Vincent, combine movement and gesture, role taking, and language. The resultant dramatic form, however, does not involve a predetermined shape, but rather is organically determined by the problem or issue with which the participants are grappling.

Drama is the only school subject "that begins and ends with people . . . and lives outside the textbook" (Wilks, 1973); it does not envelop a body of techniques which children must acquire (Witkin, 1974), nor, as McGregor (1976) writes, is there any central core of knowledge that must be assimilated. Drawing as it does on experience which is then related to the resolution of situations through dramatic form, drama in education is best seen as an experience rather than a subject (Davies, 1975), or in Heathcote's (1971) terms, a "system."

Drama in education is, then, seen as a way of teaching and learning, rather than a conventional school subject with definite knowledge to be acquired or skills to be learned (Robinson, 1975). The raw material with which the teacher works, writes Robinson (1975), is the child and "his immediate needs to relate to the world and other individuals around him," and his attempts to conceptualize that relationship and express it physically and through language.

The processes involved in shaping this material are according to Bolton (1971), composed of elements "common to both children's play and theatre, when the aims are to help children to learn about those feelings, attitudes and preconceptions that before the drama was experienced were too implicit for them to be aware of." The learning takes place through interaction in group situations (Sharpham, 1972; Payne, 1976) and also has to do with "the refining of those concepts [related to] interpersonal relationships" (Bolton, 1971).

Built into the rhetoric of drama teaching, however, and subscribed to widely in the literature, is the problematic notion of personal development through drama. Way (1967) argues that drama in education is "as intangible as personality itself," and is basically concerned with developing people. It is concerned, Way asserts, with the encouragement of originality and in the process helps the fulfilling of personal aspirations. If education, claims Way (1967), is concerned with individual development as education reports would suggest, drama is best seen as a way toward allowing individuals to assert their individuality. Such a role for drama, as suggested by Way, tends toward the mystical and to a large extent the unassailable. Indeed, to make claims for the personality developing toward a coherent whole through drama, warns Pick (1967), is absurd; to suggest that "it is a means of exploring subjectively the whole field of human relations is a tall order" (*Education Survey 2*, 1967).

Ultimately drama must be recognized principally as a learning process with a considerable role in making the curriculum "more exciting, relevant, and meaningful" (Fuller, 1973). Drama in education, it would appear, must confine itself to fulfilling only those curriculum roles which it manifestly can be seen to be fulfilling. The most important of these roles is its central curriculum function as a learning process.

Notes

1. The Schools Council Arts and the Adolescent Project (1968-1972) was based at the University of Exeter Institute of Education, England, and was prompted by *Schools Council Enquiry I: Young School Leavers* (1968) which presented a report of secondary pupils' poor evaluation of their music, art, and drama lessons. The project proposed, after a period of study and research, to offer the "prospect of a language which would enable arts teachers better to understand and control their work; a language that would have to be equally applicable to all the arts. This language would emerge as part of a more far reaching study of the educational function of the arts based on original work in the psychology of effect, on which Robert Witkin [director of research for the project] was already engaged" (Ross, 1975). As well as the "language" it was also intended that the project would produce a work of "fundamental significance to education."

Arts and the Adolescent (Ross, 1975) and *The Intelligence of Feeling* (Witkin, 1974), were the principal outcomes of the project, and to quote Ross, "it is now for arts teachers themselves to judge the value of our work and to use it to bring about such changes as they would like to see."

2. The Schools Council Drama Teaching Project (10-16) (1974-1977) was based at Goldsmiths' College, University of London. The project was established: "(i) to undertake research with a view to the clarification of aims, methods and possible ways of assessing outcomes for the main approaches to drama teaching; (ii) to produce suggested models of organisation, and teachers' guides describing work done within the main approaches to drama teaching; and (iii) to produce dissemination material to demonstrate different approaches to drama teaching and ways of evaluating drama work" (Schools Council Information Sheet).

Three films titled *Take Three* were produced to illustrate the work of the project as was the report text *Learning Through Drama* (McGregor, Tate, & Robinson, 1977).

References

Allen, J. (1955). Preface. In E. J. Burton (Ed.), *Drama in Schools*. London: Jenkins.

Allen, J. (1975). "Notes on a Definition of Drama." In J. Hodgson & M. Banham (Eds.), *Drama in Education 3*. London: Pitman.

Barnes, D. (Ed.). (1968). *Drama in the English Classroom*. Dartmouth Seminar Papers: National Council of Teachers of English.

Bolton, G. (1971). "In Search of Aims and Objectives." *Creative Drama, 4* (2), 5-8.

Britton, J., & Scott, G. (1970). *Language and Learning*. London: Penguin.

Brossell, G. C. (1975). "Researching Drama: A Humanistic Perspective." In N. Stephenson & D. Vincent (Eds.), *Teaching and Understanding Drama. London: National Foundation for Educational Research.*

Burton, E. J. (1955). *Drama in Schools*. London: Jenkins.

Clarke, M. (1977, July 8). "What is Creative?" *Times Educational Supplement*, No. 3240.

Clegg, D. (1973). "The Dilemma of Drama in Education." *Theatre Quarterly, 3* (9), 31-42.

Cook, C. (1917). *The Play Way*. London: Heinemann.

Courtney, R. (1968). *Play, Drama and Thought*. London: Cassell.

Creber, J. W. P. (1965). *Sense and Sensitivity, the Philosophy and Practice of English Teaching*. London: University of London Press.

Davies, A. (1975). *Report of Teacher Training Conference*. Schools Council Drama Teaching Project (10-16). Unpublished manuscript.

Dixon, J. (1967). *Growth Through English*. Oxford: Oxford University Press.

Education Survey 2: Drama. (1967). London: Her Majesty's Stationery Office.

England, A. W. (1976). "Where Should We Go: Educational Drama—The State of Play." *Uses of English, 27* (3), 9-16.

Fuller, R. M. (1973). *Creative Dramatics: Instructional Methodologies for the Elementary Curriculum*. Unpublished doctoral dissertation, The Ohio State University, Columbus.

Heathcote, D. (1971). "Drama in Education: Subject or System." In N. Dodd & W. Hickson (Eds.), *Drama and Theatre in Education*. London: Heinemann.

Hodgson, J., & Banham, M. (1972). "Living on Borrowed Time." In J. Hodgson & M. Banham (Eds.), *Drama* in Education I. London: Pitman.

Jennings, S. (1973). *Remedial Drama.* London: Pitman.

Jordan, D. (1967). "Movement and Drama." In J. Britton (Ed.), *The Arts in Education.* London: Harrap.

Laban, R. (1960). *The Mastery of Movement.* London: MacDonald and Evans.

Landy, R. J. (1975). *Dramatic Education: An Interdisciplinary Approach to Learning.* Unpublished doctoral dissertation, University of California, Santa Barbara.

Langer, S. (1953). *Feeling and Form.* London: Routledge and Kegan Paul.

Lee, J. (1967). *Foreword in Education Survey 2: Drama.* London: Her Majesty's Stationery Office.

McGregor, L. (1976). *Developments in Drama Teaching.* London: Open Books.

McGregor, L., Tate, M., & Robinson, K. (1977). *Learning Through Drama.* London: Heinemann.

Norman, J. L. (1971). "The Secondary Specialist." *Speech and Drama, 20* (1).

Payne, P. (1976). "Where We Are: Educational Drama— The State of Play." *Use of English, 27* (3), 5-9.

Pick, J. (1967). "A Little Food for Thought." *English in Education, 1* (3), 58-62.

Primary Education in Scotland Report. (1965). Edinburgh, Scotland: Her Majesty's Stationery Office.

Pythian, B. (1975, February 28). "Without Feeling, Music is Dead." *The Teacher, 26* (9).

Robinson, K. (1975). *Find a Space* (A Report on the Teaching of Drama). University of London Schools Examination Department. Unpublished manuscript.

Ross, M. (1972, September 22). "Cooling the Arts Curriculum." *Times Educational Supplement,* No. 2991.

Ross, M. (1975). *Arts and the Adolescent.* London: Evans/Methuen.

Rugg, H., & Shumaker, A. (1928). *The Child-Centered School.* New York: World Book.

Schools Council Enquiry I: Young School Leavers. (1968). London: Her Majesty's Stationery Office.

Scott, G. (c. 1975). *Origins and Development of Creative Drama in England.* Unpublished manuscript.

Sharpham, J. R. (1972). *A Descriptive Study of Creative Drama at Second Level in England.* Unpublished doctoral dissertation, University of Colorado.

Slade, P. (1954). *Child Drama.* University of London Press.

Stenhouse, L. (1975). *Introduction to Curriculum Research and Development.* London: Heinemann.

Stephenson, N., & Vincent, D. (Eds.). (1975). *Teaching and Understanding Drama.* London: U. K. National Foundation for Educational Research.

Stone, A. L. (1949). *Story of a School.* London: Ministry of Education (Education Pamphlet 14). London: Her Majesty's Stationery Office.

Way, B. (1967). *Development Through Drama.* London: Longmans.

Wilks, B. (1973). "Beyond the Known." In J. Hodgson & M. Banham (Eds.) *Drama in Education 2.* London: Pitman.

Witkin, R. (1974). *The Intelligence of Feeling.* London: Heinemann.

Chapter 8

DANCE IN THE SCHOOLS: A PERSONAL ACCOUNT

Moira Logan

The perspectives I bring are grounded in my experiences in the studio and the classroom, particularly my experience as an artist in the schools. While scholars generally work in the clean, reasonable, and weightless world of ideas, teachers work in classrooms which have their own gravity and are seldom clean and never reasonable. The classroom is a mutable space—a cauldron of dynamic energies. It has this in common with dance—this changing, quicksilver, difficult-to-grab-hold-of quality. In this sense dance and education should be natural allies.

Nowhere is this more apparent than in the elementary grades. This same changeability, this sense of becoming, of inventing yourself and the world as you go along, are also the hallmarks of childhood. Children are natural movers, literally wiggling and squirming with an excess of energy, startling us with the grace and beauty of their spontaneous movement-play. What more fitting way for children to harness their energy and imagination than to give form to that movement expression—to dance?

Many teachers recognize this, but do not understand enough about dance and are too uncomfortable with it themselves to do anything about it. Consequently, apart from a few arts magnet schools that employ dance specialists, opportunities for children to encounter dance in a school setting are rare. The current (one hopes stop-gap) solution to this problem is a variety of state and local artist-in-the-schools programs. Some of these are performance oriented; others have a workshop format involving children in participatory dance experiences.

THE ARTIST-IN-THE-SCHOOLS PROGRAM

The Ohio State University's artist-in-the-schools program is sponsored by the Greater Columbus Arts Council and tours schools throughout central Ohio. The intent is to introduce ideas about dance as an art form. Ideas about space, time, and energy are illustrated with dance improvisations and related short works in a way that children can understand and relate to. The works themselves are from the company's repertory. The performances are interactive; the audience responds to questions and may ask their own questions. At other times they are participatory; the children may move in place, clapping out rhythms and moving their bodies along with the dancers.

In one session audience members are invited to join with the dancers in guided movement. Children and company members collaborate doing a variety of locomotor paterns and creating designs in space. This is good for general hilarity and camaraderie and allows children to explore for themselves what it is to balance, to create their own body shapes, to extend into space, to contract, to melt to the floor and spiral up again—in short to move with both freedom and control.

My role in this process is to teach a follow-up lesson in dance. The landscape of ideas which were presented visually and verbally in the lecture-demonstration now becomes the children's own territory—their own field of exploration and discovery. We begin the lesson in the time-honored fashion—sitting in a circle on the floor and discussing the performance. Someone mentions an exciting piece of virtuosity. Someone else remembers a tender lyrical part, another a dynamic, dramatic dance. The children talk about the dances and dancers which have moved them and which, in turn, make them want to move.

Then we begin to explore, to experiment with rhythms and shapes, with gestures and traveling patterns. The process is the important part—discovering the variety of ways to approach a movement idea. Without benefit of a story and with only the accompaniment of small percussion instruments, the emphasis is on movement itself and the motivation to move comes from the pleasure of kinesthetic or physical involvement.

At this stage technique, or skill development for its own sake, is not an issue. The need for skill evolves in relation to the desire for a more precise and refined form of expression. The lesson develops sequentially, one movement idea building upon another, each one extending and amplifying the one before, until an entire phrase or dance study is created through the combined efforts of the children and teacher.

Reprinted with permission from *Theory Into Practice*, Autumn 1984. © 1984 by the College of Education, The Ohio State University.

There are many possibilities. We may begin by exploring round, angular, and twisted body shapes, the formulating a statement which begins with a curved body design followed by a spiraling movement through space which resolves momentarily in a twisted pretzel-like shape. From this comes an unwinding and the climax of the phrase—a running and leaping gesture which pierces the space, ending the statement with a sudden, dynamic freeze.

Each class unfolds differently and has its own rhythm. A lesson on gestures and sounds draws from one of the dances in the performance which makes use of everyday gesture and vocalization. The class follows with a warm-up based on the gestures of reaching and grasping which then develops into twisting and wringing and finally into traveling and turning. A gesture may be transferred from a hand to a leg, from an elbow to a knee, from high to low, all the time changing in timing and quality. Abstraction is the word used to describe the way in which the everyday gesture is transformed into dance movement, removed from the ordinary into the realm of the aesthetic.

Sound and movement are elements to be explored together. The familiar human sounds of sighing, laughing, or crying are coupled with movement, amplified and exaggerated until they become larger than life. After more vocalization the children are ready to compose their own vocal score which becomes the accompaniment for a dance based on gesture. The class is divided into groups and each group evolves its own dance—some with an element of humor and whimsy, others in a more serious or dramatic vein.

VALUE FOR EDUCATION

The value of these dance experiences is that the world of dance, the aesthetic dimension of movement, is demystified for the children; it is available and open to them. Having tested their own skills and created their own dances, they are better able to understand and appreciate what the dance performer or choreographer must do to create dance and bring it to an audience. Knowing what is involved in making and performing dance enables them to look at it with sharpened perception and insight. At least that is the aim.

While dance may be an eloquent art form, it is nevertheless an inarticulate one that may not lend itself to the usual modes of cognitive investigation. This sometimes makes it difficult for students to gain ready access to it, especially in an educational system that values more linear approaches to learning. Like the other arts, dance gives us access to a nonverbal metaphoric dimension of experience, one that has to be experienced to be understood; and yet, once children go beyond the early elementary grades, this mode of learning is neglected and ignored.

Kinesthesia, our sense of movement, is in my view the mediating link between our inner world of psychic experience and the outer world of objects and events.

This sense of movement is pathetically undereducated and thus quickly overwhelmed by those senses which more clearly serve the rational, analytical aspects of human consciousness.

John Dewey, whose ideas still reverberate throughout education, was an enthusiastic student and proponent of the discoveries of F. M. Alexander, whose life's work dealt with the education of the kinesthetic sense. Alexander, an Australian actor faced with severe vocal difficulties, set out to discover and eliminate in his own body the patterns of tension which were the source of his problem. In so doing, he developed a method for enhancing kinesthetic awareness and increasing physical freedom.

Dewey, in an attempt to come to terms with the mind-body dichotomy of his day, concluded that "men are afraid, without even being aware of their fear to recognize the most wonderful of all the structures of the universe—the human body" (Maisel, 1969, p. xiv). He believed Alexander's ideas had relevance for education. In fact, the Alexander method remedies problems which might never arise if children were given a kinesthetic education which matched the visual and verbal education traditionally provided by schools. Unfortunately Dewey's ideas on the education of the kinesthetic sense have escaped notice within education.

A refinement of the kinesthetic sense is basic to the dance experience. Both doing and responding to dance require a fundamental appreciation of how movement happens and what it feels like. To perceive subtle changes in the use of energy, to respond to dynamic rhythms, to sense the emotional textures of movement, to be aware of space as a tangible entity—these are sensibilities that can be nurtured through dance.

The realm of sensory experience, which includes the whole rich and diverse spectrum of sense impressions, forms the basis for aesthetic experience. The artist draws upon sensory resources in creating; the audience, in responding. The sensations of movement are fundamental and go beyond the functional considerations of locating your body in space and having an accurate impression of how much force it may take to twist the lid off a jar of peanut butter, hammer a picture hook into the wall, or shift from second to third gear. In this going beyond the everyday, the unique character of the dance is disclosed and a range of meanings made possible.

When movement activities and the sensations of moving are connected to the expressive and imaginative powers of the mover, dance begins to happen. Dance and its appreciation involve a heightened kinesthetic awareness, a bodily intelligence, and a sharpened perception of movement as a dimension of aesthetic experience.

References

Maisel, E. (1969). *The Resurrection of the Body*. New York: Dell Publishing.

Chapter 9

BODY MOVEMENT AND LEARNING

Robert E. Gensemer

Actually, it was all Rudolph Laban's doing. Laban was born in Germany and spent his early life in that country. When his ideas were not well received there, he found solace in England where he became the pioneer of movement education.

Laban believed that physical movement could be an expression of life itself. He considered it the most viable means for discovering one's self and one's existence with the world. Human beings, he said, were "total" only when they were moving. The multiple variables of thought, feeling, and will could only be combined in a movement medium.

No one understood movement education at first. Many people thought it was just another name for modern dance, which it was not. Others saw it as merely another way to teach gymnastics, which it was originally. The early confusion came from misinterpretations of Laban's ideas. Some of his writings (see especially Laban 1948 and 1960) have great existentialistic overtones and often do remind one of modern dance. Further, the provisions for learning which are characteristic of movement education are readily applied through gymnastics. It has taken some time to apprehend the real meaning of what Laban was telling us. It appears that he was actually speaking about the reticular formation, as well as about kinesthesis and biofeedback—not in the same terminology or even the same thought, but in substance.

FOUR DIMENSIONS OF MOVEMENT

Laban analyzed movement from the standpoint of certain principles, only four of which he believed warranted attention: *space, weight, time,* and *flow.* Laban regarded all movement as a blending, in various degrees, of these four qualities. Descriptively, they are as follows:

1. *Space.* Essentially, this quality refers to the manner in which movement uses an area. Laban first thought of it as either an economic quality of "personal space," which is that area within reach of an individual; or the more expansive consideration of "general space," which is everywhere else. Additionally, the body can move in space in different directions, in different pathways, at different levels, or in different shapes. Thus, the baseball pitcher contorts into a series of movements within the realm of personal space, and the batter who hits and runs and slides is using general space with all its variances.

2. *Weights.* As the term might imply, this quality is the degree of muscular tension involved in movement. It may be strong, resistant, and forceful; or it may be relaxed, light, and easy. When you chop firewood on Saturday morning you use movements of different weight from those used when you play golf that afternoon.

3. *Time.* This is a quality of tempo. A movement can be slow or fast. This factor also includes the amplitudes of being sudden and abbreviated or progressive and sustained. The speed of movement can also change throughout, becoming faster or slower. A tennis forehand normally involves a movement which increases in impulse as the ball is hit, although it could also be intentionally slowed. Moreover, the time of a movement can be a series of rhythmical changes, as is so true in dance.

4. *Flow.* This is the aspect of the fluency of movement. It may be "bound," meaning movement which can be stopped and held without much difficulty, as in many wrestling maneuvers; or it may be a flailing abandon, as in the gyrations of a discus thrower.

The important feature of all these qualities is not so much the definitions or differences but the fact that differences in movement dimensions exist. Laban realized this fact. He was simply trying to delineate the variables and give direction to teaching. Over the years Laban's ideas have often been misunderstood, misjudged, fanaticized, overestimated, underestimated, and otherwise maligned. His main objective was to make us aware that learners move in various dimensions and that the essence of teaching and self-appropriated learning is to attend to all the variables.

FROM INNER SPACE TO OUTER SPACE

Some authors have considered these variables as the foundation of a program of "basic movement." From this point of view, efficiency of movement is assumed to develop from an initial learning of the how, what, and where of motor activity. A kinesthetic recognition and voluntary control of changes serve as the motoric ground floor for later refinement of movement patterns. The

Adapted from *Movement Education.*© 1979 by the National Education Association.

contention is that learners need to enhance (or recapture) the natural biological relations between the proprioceptive sense and the cognitive awareness of it. Consequently, in a designed program of movement education, the first experiences are oriented toward a stimulus of the basic differences in movement qualities. This procedure is very similar in context to Jacobson's method of teaching relaxation.

The teacher of such basic movement awareness may wish to select an organizational theme and give most of the attention to the theme during classes. For example, a sample lesson for the concept of space for children might proceed somewhat like the following illustration which is an adaptation of lessons suggested by Gilliom (1970, pp. 54–60):

Begin by having the children seated on the floor, each child in an area where s/he cannot reach out and touch another. The first series of explorations do not require children to move away from their areas. The verbalizations given are merely suggestive of movements to be evoked and are not to be taken as absolutes or complete possibilities.

1. Move one hand around you, reaching as many places as you can.

2. Now, move the other hand around. Can you find some space with this hand that you cannot find with your other one?

3. Move both hands around, finding as much of your own space as you can. Is there space near you? far away? as much in back of you as in front?

4. Now, move only your head. Does your head move in the same way as your hands? Can you move your head to as many places as you could move your hands? Can you use the rest of your body to help you move your head, while still staying seated?

5. Now, let's all try moving just one foot around. Move it into as much space as you can. Can you take it as many places as you could take your hands? How can you move your foot around you without touching the floor? Can you get it high above you? Now, try all these things with your other foot.

6. Here's a strange one. Put your head on the floor, and see how many places you can move the rest of your body.

7. Now, you will need to listen carefully, because there will be some changes for you to make without stopping any of your movements. Start by moving one hand around you again, as you did before. Now, move the other hand so that both hands are moving. Stretch as far as you can without getting up. Can you make it seem as if you are touching alot of space around you? And now, make your two hands go in two different directions at the same time. Can one hand go in straight lines

while the other goes in circles? Keep your hands moving and, now, move your head at the same time. Can you add one foot to all this movement? And, then, the other foot? Are you moving as many parts of you as you can into as many places as you can?

In these early movement explorations, sufficient time must be provided for each student to experience each of the suggestions. Taking too much time between the verbal stimuli is preferable to taking too little, particularly since the time interval may actually allow for some cognitive perceptions of the movements.

Also, it is good to circulate among students while giving the verbalizations since it may be necessary to make individual suggestions here and there to those having difficulty inventing changes in their movement patterns.

8. Now, put both hands on the floor and see how many ways you can move your body around your hands. Keep both hands glued to the floor all the time. Can you get your feet very close to your hands? very far away? Can you get one of your feet above you? both feet?

9. Now, lie on your back. Can you try some of the same movements? Touch your hands to your feet. Now, get them as far away from each other as you can. Roll over to lie on your stomach. Can you reach your hands or feet into the space that is now above you? Is this the same space that is behind you when you are standing?

10. Now, stand up. Keep one foot on the ground, as if it were nailed there, and use all parts of your body to find and reach into all the space around you. Can you reach into high space? low space? Can you twist your body around to touch the space that is behind you?

11. Touch the floor, now, with both feet and one hand. Reach all around your space. Is it smaller than it was before? Touch only one foot and one hand to the floor. How does this change your movements? Try balancing on one foot, and then reach all around you, high, low, and to the sides. Put both your knees on the floor and do the same thing. Now, use any two parts of your body that you haven't used before to support your weight. Use two different parts this time. Now, use only one part of your body to support your weight. Use a body part other than your feet. Can you use one body part that you haven't used before?

This beginning motor experimentation is intended to generate an initial kinesthetic sensitivity to the basic changes and possibilities of bodily movements. in space. As is true with all nonstructured problems, the movement responses may be quite varied, and all the variances could be correct. This is simply a result of the fact that open-ended suggestion are subject to diverse interpretations. For example, if the children are lying on their backs and the suggestion is given to "reach your arms high," some students may extend their arms upward toward the ceiling, while others may stretch their arms beyond the top of their heads, parallel with the floor. Both responses are acceptable in the minds of students.

What is more important than individual interpretations of any single problem is the *variability* that each student can demonstrate. All students should be able to execute a number of different ways of accomplishing the same end. And they should be able to alter the responses at will with a full recognition of whether or not they have previously used a particular pattern. The simple suggestion "Now, do it a different way" should evoke a new response for the same problem from each of the students. Some may not be able to make such distinctions and instead will persist in movement patterns which resemble previous ones. In this case, if further verbal suggestions do not seem to elicit varied responses, it may be well to have these students watch others, not for the purpose of imitation but to give them a visual suggestion to go along with the auditory input they have already received.

Next, students can move into a more general utilization of space.

12. Now, we're going to use the big space that is all around you in this room (or a defined area outside). Let's all move around in this big space, going to all parts of it. Try to keep away from everyone else as you move around. How many different ways can you move through this space? Try something different from running. Can you move backward? sideways? fast? slow? high? low?

13. See if you can get your feet very high as you move. How high can you get your whole body? Is there something you can do with your arms to help you get your whole body into the air? Can your knees be higher than your hips when you are in the air? Are there different things you can do when in the air?

14. Try to be in a stretched position as you move around the room. Now, be very small as you move. Can you move by using your hands and feet together on the floor? Can you go from one place to another by having both feet land on the floor at the same time? And here's a difficult one — can you move around from one place to another without touching your feet or hands to the floor?

Students should be using all the space, not just part of it. Again, there should be a versatility shown by each of the students. Sometimes it may be helpful to have half the class observe the other half, or one student who is particularly inventive might be asked to show the movement possibilities to the entire class.

To add another dimension, children could be asked to "freeze" into a static position on a given sig-

nal (a word or clap of hands). This variation offers them a chance to have a "stop-action" still photograph of the patterns they are executing — a visual representation of their actions. Thus, they can inspect their responses and gain additional information regarding their production of movement.

TALKING TO THE BODY

The real advantage of movement education is the new dimension it adds to mind-body interactions. There is the development of a psychodynamic energy which can constantly gauge the voltage of muscle activity. The mind becomes capable of responding directly and specifically to the information it is being fed by the dancing of hundreds of thousands of muscle cell impulses.

That's only part of the story, however. In the final act, the mind can *alter* the states of muscle events to satisfy the moment-by-moment demands. The mind not only receives information, it also sends information.

Exactly how does one get to the final step of *telling* the muscles how to work? Movement education intends to teach people not only how to *receive* information but also how to *use* that information to affect motor responses. How can this best be done?

For one thing, we must communicate with the body in language it understands. the body does not really know English or French or Esperanto. Its native language is *feeling*. It communicates by *sensation*. Consequently, if we talk to the body in normal verbalizations, those verbalizations must get translated into sensations before they can be understood. Thus, we cannot necessarily *tell* the body what to do in the same way that we can talk to another person about math or history or the weather.

Even in those moments when we liberate our minds for the pure brainstorming of daydreaming, we tend to channel our thoughts into language. Yet when we want to execute a motor performance, words can get in the way. If we want a strike in the tenth frame, we cannot talk the body into it by saying, "OK, body, do your pushaway first. Then take the ball back on the second step, keep your shoulders straight, your eyes on the target, bring the ball on a direct line for that target, and follow through." Instead, we must simply ask the body to send the ball into the pocket.

We start by not using words, or at least by using as few as possible. Rather, we must use *images*. We must imagine our performance. We must *see* it and *feel* it as we see it. And that's a nonverbal affair. There is no language that can describe it. We do it without any need for words.

And so here we are with a group of thirty students in front of us, whom we are trying to help use their bodies better. We've got to say *something* to them. We can't just stand there without using any words at all. As soon as we say something, however, we run the risk that the words we use to describe any movement will get bounced around in thirty brains and come out with thirty different interpretations. We can't say to all students, "Keep your left arm straight," if we are teaching them how to hit a golf ball, expecting that it has the same connotation for everyone. What is *straight*? Is it a locked arm? Is it a comfortably extended arm? Is it a hyperextended arm?

Furthermore, there is enough evidence (see especially Marteniuk 1976) to let us know that the more a teacher verbalizes about the "how" of motor execution, the more student perceptions tend to be drawn into mechanical ways of thinking about motor events. It may even be better, in the teaching of certain motor performances, to simply demonstrate the execution and say *nothing* about the mechanics. In this way, each student can receive the stimulus of the demonstration with his/her own reference system — an individually private way to sense the movement with personal physiological language. Such a procedure is a nonverbal means of communicating about a nonverbal event.

Yet, the matter isn't quite so simple. Any teacher who wishes to enhance student perceptions of the sensory aspects of motor performance must intentionally direct attention to those aspects. Words are required. This is the real reason why the teaching technique of movement education is verbally *suggestive* and why it *allows* individual interpretation of the words. This technique is a safeguard against the potential misrepresentation of verbal communication.

Thus, the important teaching factor in movement education is to supply the body with *meaningful* information. Since the methodology is based on exploration, problem solving, and self-appropriated learnings, the information provided by the teacher must necessarily be open-ended. This is another reminder that the art of movement education is to be a stimulator rather than a dictator.

References

Gilliom, Bonnie Cherp. *Basic Movement Education for Children: Rationale and Teaching Units*. Reading, Mass.: Addison-Wesley Publishing Co., 1970.

Laban, Rudolph. *Modern Educational Dance*. London: MacDonald and Evans, 1948.

——. *The Mastery of Movement*. 2nd ed. Revised by Lisa Ullman. London: MacDonald and Evans, 1960.

Marteniuk, Ronald G. *Information Processing in Motor Skills*. New York: Holt, Rinehart and Winston, 1976.

Chapter 10

THE PERFORMANCE OF LITERATURE

Lee Hudson and Beverly Whitaker Long

If we predated this essay to focus on the early 1930's, we could settle into a discussion of the "oral interpretation of literature" and its fairly recent name change from "oral expression" and the "vocal interpretation of literature." We would enjoy the comforts of a generally widespread consensus on what oral interpretation or interpretative reading should accomplish and how. Interpretation, then well-flanked by the aesthetics of conventions, could handily be defined either by what it was (the re-creation and communication of literature) or by what it was not (acting, impersonation, and public speaking).

The last 50 years, however, have seen these particular determinants steadily fade. To investigate this large shift in perspective, we will proceed from a brief historical overview to an outline of current theory and practice, suggesting implications for today. In this essay we use the words *interpretation* and *performance* interchangeably although a distinction can be made between interpretation as a perspective and performance as a perspective rendered.

THE AMERICAN TRADITION OF INTERPRETATION

When the National Association of Academic Teachers of Public Speaking was formed in 1914, the elocutionary influence on public address and oral reading began to slowly dissolve. The earlier-formulated expression theory emerged with an insistence that the *internal* realization of literature govern its *external* presentation, supplanting the elocutionist's frequent reverse emphasis on proper delivery techniques. Guided by an aesthetic of minimalism or suggestion, readers could, thus, share literature with others while simultaneously developing their own inner resources. The second two decades of the century were not literature-oriented times but rather, in their own divergent ways, both insisted on the performer's physical, mental, or spiritual growth, and literature provided a more or less satisfactory vehicle for this improvement.

While some serious consideration of the literature did exist earlier among a few writers, the 30's and 40's brought rationales grounded in literary theory for reading and its communication to others. Interpretation began what was to become a pattern up to the present day—the application of methods current in literary criticism to the students' purpose for oral reading and their preparation of materials. In the 40's that methodology was not as consistent as it would be later. As yet, readers still wrote a precis or paraphase of the selection in a general search for the author's central meaning—a practice soon to fall under the heavy fire of the New Critics who provided vocabulary and a method for examining the specifics of a literary text.

In the 50's interpretation educators voiced dissatisfaction with the terms *readings* and *recitations,* and with the lifeless, unintelligent renderings these descriptors implied. Instead, they developed a fuller conceptualization of interpretation, one that considered performances as critical explorations or textual illuminations of a literary selection. It was a short, but crucial, step to then view the performance itself as a demonstrated act of literary criticism offering unique critical insight. Performance as criticism combined the detachment of an objective, analytical, critical method with the engagement inhrent in a performer's directly experiential approach. *Performance as knowing* became the key concept dominating, in one way or another, the contributions made during the 60's. An important transition was just beginning: Presentation, oral reading, representation, expression, recitation, or interpretation was evolving into the fuller concept of *performed literature*. Probably because it conjured up thoughts of trivial activity, impersonation, or acting, the word *performance* did not popularly, or even casually, appear in interpretation literature until the 1960's. Diversity within the field was identifiable as teachers began developing their areas of emphasis: the *reader's* growth (technically as a performer or humanistically as a person); the *audience's* understanding and enjoyment of the shared literature; or the study of *literature* through the medium of performance.

Adapted from *Education in the 80's: Speech Communication.* © 1981 by the National Education Association.

The late 60's and the 70's added the dynamics of the concept of performance to the textual implications of New Criticism. Instead of criticism's leading a reader from understanding to presenting, performance was insisting on its simultaneous textual ontology: The text *was* its performance. With each performance the literature was being redefined. The meaning of *performance* in its basic sense—to bring a thing to completion—reminds us that to comprehend is to perform, in a sense. We perform when we realize, recognize, and understand the integrated emotional and cognitive dimensions of the literary text. A vocal-physical- psychical performance, then, expands to encompass our sense of all three contexts—social, literary, and personal. Naturally a public performance will involve a social sensibility conditioned by audience identity and purpose. The literary context introduces consideration of both the literary speaker's audience and the author's historical audience. A personal context, in addition, governs the development of a student's highly individual encounter with literature.

THEORY AND PRACTICE FOR TODAY AND TOMORROW

With neither crystal ball nor prophetic powers to spin out developments in the teaching of interpretation tomorrow, we can only examine the salient strengths of the present and outline what is likely to happen, to continue, or to intensify if educators persist in believing—as we think they will—that performance is a challenging and worthwhile way of studying literature. The items we will comment on include basic philosophical objectives and the movement of performance from the speech communication classroom to other settings.

Basic Philosophical Objectives

The basic objective of performance as literary study is closely tied to the root meaning of the word *perform*: execute, fulfill, complete, furnish, finish. In each case, the lower life synonym is simply *do*. And why this "doing" of literature? The reason lies in the interest of knowing or, better still, in a knowing/feeling of those experiences expressed in literary texts. Such a thesis claims that performance, central to the whole literary process, is more fully realized if the reader actually "tries on" what the literature notates by performing it (doing, actualizing, acting, being, etc.).

Louise Rosenblatt, a noted English educator, claims that a written piece of literature is a *text* and that a *poem* (or any literature) exists only as a transaction occurs between *reader* and text.[1] The print on the page, thus, becomes an experience in literature only when a person—or persons—makes connection with it.

If an even more basic goal is needed, we can borrow one from Walter Ong, S.J., who writes: "Acting a role, realizing in a specially intense way one's identity (in a sense) with someone who (in another sense) one is not, remains one of the most human things a person can do."[2] The potential liberalizing effect of this "realizing in a specially intense way" is not yet scientifically measurable; however, it is a firmly held commitment (and one that is confirmed almost daily) for most teachers and students of liberal and performing arts, and the conviction seems likely to grow even more secure in the future.

Performance in Special Situations

Even for those who find the raison d'être for interpretation in its value to literary study, the time comes when teachers have an opportunity to take performing techniques and/or performances outside their own classroom for different or wider audiences. The most common example occurs when the teacher's aims move from the literary growth of the individual through the *process* of performance to an interest in performance as *product* for the understanding and enjoyment of an audience. Ordinarily labeled readers' theatre or chamber theatre, these group performances face most of the same problems as do other theatrical events: a playing space, adequate facilities, budget, copyright, programs, costumes, etc. Although these performances are not generally expected to be as lavish as traditional theatre (largely because the Aristotelian element of "spectacle" is rarely emphasized or even attempted), the teacher still faces responsibility for ensuring the audience insofar as possible, an aesthetically engaging and satisfying time in the theatre. Inadequately prepared theatre, regardless of its label, is only minimally educational. Certainly not meant to discourage public performances by interpreters, this assertion is intended only to suggest that enterprises appropriate to the classroom may disappoint public audiences who have reason to expect a finished and carefully honed production, the kind implicitly promised by the invitation or advertisement. Interpretation teachers' effectiveness may be greatly strengthened by training in theatre and allied arts; their directing of productions demands it, formally or informally.

Another kind of performance outside the classroom now enjoying a resurgence in popularity occurs in specialized social contexts: prisons, hospitals, recreation centers, retirement homes, and discussion groups, for example. Used as entertainment or as illustrative material for lecture-discussions led by an expert, these peformances can be meaningful for performers and listeners.

Teachers interested in performance as a service to other groups should look for opportunities within their own school system: having reading hours to promote library week; giving dramatized readings of famous debates for a history course; reading poems for elementary school children who are interested in composing their own; and performing innumerable selections for English classes about to begin a given unit of study.

A less obvious connection just starting to be explored also occurs in English classrooms, but with a decidedly different emphasis (and one that is especially exciting for the teacher of speech communication). As a result of the important studies made by the National Council of Teachers of English in the late 60's, English education programs have been exploring ways in which solo performances in class, oral reading exercises, and group interpretation activities enhance student understanding and enjoyment of literature. Most recently, reading acquisition and composition programs have been investigating the influence of performance behaviors on written communication competency. If we absorb the vocabulary, grammar, and rhythms of language through speech (initially in childhood and throughout life), then oralizing and internalizing expressive language from our literature in a performance situation could well extend our language sensibilities and usage. Thus, interpretation teachers may be centrally involved in the return of joint programs in oral and written English.

CONCLUSION

The ensuing discussion reveals our commitment, first and foremost, to the humanistic impulse—in the belief that here is where interpretation most properly can make a major contribution to students whose present and future lives may be significantly enriched by full encounters with literature. Moreover, of the speech communication arts and sciences, interpretation is, perhaps, the most humanistically oriented and, thus, able to make important and unique contributions to the field of speech communication as a whole.

In short, we affirm the humanness, even the naturalness, of literary study and the possibilities of insight through literature in performance. Literature, both on the page and in performance, merits our students' careful attention—even what Richard McGuire calls *passionate* attention. In the introduction to *Passionate Attention: An Introduction to Literary Study,* he explains:

I see the acts of living and of reading and studying literature as having value only if they are motivated by love and interest; passionate attention is thus the richest short description of literary criticism I know. It represents the most important human qualities involved in a person's relationships with other persons and with literature.[3]

If we add to his acts "of living . . . reading and studying literature" the acts of attending to performances in and of texts, we may say with him that "passionate attention" is the "richest short description" available for what we envision for the performance of literature in the future.

References

1. Rosenblatt, Louise. *The Text, The Poem: The Transactional Theory of the Literary Work.* Carbondale: Southern Illinois University Press, 1978.

2. Ong, Walter, S.J., as cited in: Gibson, Walker. *Persona: A Style Study for Readers and Writers.* New York: Random House, 1968.

3. McGuire, Richard. *Passionate Attention: An Introduction to Literary Study.* New York: W. W. Norton, 1973.

Additional Readings

Bacon, Wallace A. *The Art of Interpretation.* Third edition. New York: Holt, Rinehart and Winston, 1979.

————, and Breen, Robert. *Literature as Experience.* New York: McGraw-Hill, 1959.

Beloof, Robert L. *The Performing Voice in Literature.* Boston: Little, Brown, and Co., 1966.

Doyle, Esther M., and Floyd, Virginia Hastings. *Studies in Interpretation.* Amsterdam: Rodopi NV, vol. I—1972, vol. II—1978.

Geiger, Don. *The Sound, Sense, and Performance of Literature.* Chicago: Scott, Foresman and Co., 1963.

Roloff, Leland H. *The Perception and Evocation of Literature.* Glenview, Ill.: Scott, Foresman and Co., 1973.

Chapter 11

THE FIRST SONGS OF SUMMER

David I. Steinberg and Judith E. Traub

I wish she would come back to me.
'Cause she sure 'nough will be my star.
So little shining star,
No matter where you go, you're mine.
You're my shining star.

A fourteen-year-old boy with learning disabilities wrote the lyrics quoted above. He and 19 other junior high age students were involved in an experimental class designed to teach songwriting in a 6-week summer session at the Kingsbury Lab School, a private school in Washington, D.C., for children with learning disabilities.

We began by believing that everyone could write songs. The first day it was important to write a song as a group, to play it together, and to have it sound terrific.

"How many of you have never played a xylophone before?" asked Dave.

Four hands slowly raised.
"You'll be able to play today."
Judy passed out the xylophones. The students tried them out. On a large sheet of poster board, Dave wrote:

<u>C E G</u>

Pointing to the letters, Dave said, "Pick a note, any note."

Marty Yelled, "C!"

Dave wrote a "C" under the first group of letters, and added a new group.

<u>C E G</u>   <u>G B D</u>
C

"We have the first note of our song. Who wants to pick the next one?"

"B!"

Dave added a "B" under the second group. When we had finished, there were four notes chosen from four different groups. It looked like this:

<u>C E G</u>   <u>G B D</u>   <u>C E G</u>   <u>G B D</u>
C   B   G   D

Then Bobby asked, "Which 'C'?"

"There are two 'C's' on a xylophone," said Dave, "a high one and a low one. Which one sounds best to you?"

"The low one."

"O.K., here's how you write it on a music card." Dave drew a box and put a "C" in it and said, "You put a low 'C' near the bottom. You start it near the left because we read music from left to right, just like we read words in sentences."

The class decided where the next three notes would go and decided we should play it through twice. The card looked like this:

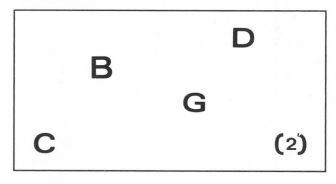

Judy wrote the songs on index cards for each student to have near him or her, and spent time helping those students who were new to the xylophone. The class practiced the song for a few minutes. Dave accompanied them on the piano, playing C and G chords in a rock and roll beat. The class was smiling. The biggest smiles came from the guys who had never played an instrument before.

"The song sounds good, but it can sound better. Let's add new instruments."

Big xylophones were set up. Drums and woodblocks were handed out. We took a few minutes to warm up. The song was played again. Now it sounded great!

"Today we wrote and played our first song as a group. See you tomorrow."

Over the next two weeks, the students wrote their own individual melodies through this same method. By using this process, they discovered that the groupings of notes were actually chords.

Adapted from *Teaching Handicapped Students English*. © 1981 by the National Education Association.

Writing their own music, the students were practicing many of the same skills they would need to construct word sentences in their other academic work. Notes had to be written in a left to right sequence and properly placed on a page. Each student was taught to write music in such a way as to designate on paper the specific position of each note in accordance with its position on a keyboard. When reading their own melodies, the students had to understand the symbolic languages used, a skill that is directly related to the reading process.

Playing our songs as a group helped make it safe for the students to write their own melodies. Next we asked them to write their own lyrics. For most students, this was a frightening assignment. To help the students be successful at lyric writing, we found several basic requirements were needed. First we discovered that we needed a large number of adults because this was to be a one-to-one experience. We were fortunate to have with us graduate students so that for each group of 10 students there were 3 adults. We had the use of several tape recorders and each student had her/his own cassette and notebook.

Our basic process was a language experience approach. Each student would work privately with one teacher and, after discussion, the student would dictate his ideas. Together they would review the song and make any desired changes. If the student had a melody in mind, he/she would sing and record the tune. That night a teacher would take home the lyric and cassette, figure out the song by ear and rewrite it so that the song could be played on the piano. The next day the teacher would play the song for the student privately so that the student could make any more desired changes. If the student gave permission, the song would be played in class. By the end of the day, a neatly written copy of the song would be placed in the student's notebook.

Sometimes a student would write about an ordinary experience like coming to school.

I really hate to wait for buses that come late.
I'd rather walk than ride.
'Cause when I do get on there's no where to sit.
And then I have a really big fit.

Sometimes a student would borrow a melody. The following song about World War III was written to the tune of "The William Tell Overture."

There once was a ship that sailed the ocean.
It was a big one with four smokestacks.
But then suddenly one day
A torpe-e-do,
With the name of the ship, hit it.

The best part of the summer happened when students expressed their feelings on issues that were important to them. Sometimes the feelings about an incident at home would be expressed in song.

When I came home and found mama
She was cryin'. I asked her what was wrong.
She said my daddy just walked out.

He said he's never comin' back.
She said, "What're we gonna do?"
And that's when I became a rock and roll star.

Some of the older students wrote love songs.

I don't know why I'm madly in love with you.
I wish I knew why I was madly in love with you.
But I maybe just have a crush on a girl like you.
You're just breakin', breakin' my heart.

One student expressed how living in the city can perhaps be a frightening experience.

What you know will not hurt you,
If you talk it out.
But if the boy finds out,
Then he will beat you to death.

It is always hard to say goodby to people you feel close to. This song was used to express feelings about separation.

I'm leavin' come tomorrow. Don't be sad. I want no sorrow.
I'll take my hell over there, and leave it there tomorrow.
I'll be back for your lovin'. You can bet your cat on that.
I'm leavin' come tomorrow, and I'll take your heart with me.

The students found it enjoyable to write satirical songs about their teachers and the school. When Dave accepted this song with good humor, the student went on to write many others. (To the tune of "Rock A Bye Baby")

Rock and roll Davey on the guitar,
When the crowd cheers, you feel you're a star.
When the strings break, you feel like a fool.
So don't worry, Davey, you can still teach at school.

The same student wrote the following verse to the tune of "Old MacDonald," and it expressed all our good feelings about our successful work and each other.

The school is proud of its kids,
And why shouldn't it be?
They're the best in this whole town,
It's easy for you to see.
They work so hard, to do their best.
Know that they can do no less.
The school is proud of its kids,
And why shouldn't it be?

Acknowledgments

First we wish to thank the students for trusting us enough to share their feelings in song. We would like to thank our graduate assistants, Nessa Spitzer and Diana Lambros, for their strong commitment to the program. We would also like to thank the administration of the Kingsbury Lab School for granting us the freedom we needed to experiment.

Chapter 12

ON THE CUTTING EDGE: MUSIC, THEATER, VISUAL ARTS

Rita Kotter
Rosina Lopez de Short
Sharon Rasor

NEA asked three classroom teachers to share their ideas and suggestions regarding how they view their special areas of fine arts education. Then, six other teachers were invited to express their reactions to those views. The composite originally appeared in the 1984-85 annual edition of *Today's Education*.

VISUAL ARTS

Through art, asserts Rosina Lopez de Short, students can learn about history, about ideas—and about themselves. Short is an art teacher at Pojoaque High School in Santa Fe, New Mexico. She feels strongly that art should be a vital part of every student's education.

I didn't start out as an art teacher. History was my subject. But over the years, and since I began teaching art full-time, I've come to the conclusion that the visual arts are a vital part of any student's education.

Through a strong arts program, students grow in visual awareness. They begin to really use their imagination, while at the same time improving their skills in producing different kinds of art works. Art education gives students opportunities to express their ideas and feelings and to learn about their own and other cultures, historical periods, and artistic styles.

Once introduced to art, students begin to sharpen their critical thinking skills. They learn to evaluate their own work by evaluating works of art from the past.

Most of my ideas for my art classes relate to history. Living in northern New Mexico, where the arts are so much a part of the culture and where a sense of history abounds, challenges me to develop programs that will awaken my students to their entire cultural heritage. The tri-cultural—Native American, Hispanic, and Anglo—backgrounds of my students provide me with many exciting ideas. One project I've developed centers on the folk art of painting the images of saints. Using this art form, which developed during the Spanish Colonial period of New Mexico's history, students learn about an artistic technique *and* the history involved in it.

This art form involves both carving images of saints (*bultos*) and painting pictures of saints (*retablos*). Using native materials—soft pine, aspen, gypsum, and natural mineral colors—religious artists created many images. For one project, I give my students instructions on technique, designs used for the borders, and a list of popular subjects, and ask them to create their own paintings. The assignment stresses simplicity of design, line, color, and drawing. One of its side benefits is that students needn't be concerned if their works are awkward or two-dimensional; early artists weren't trained specialists. As the projects progress, students have a chance to develop their own basic skills in research, writing, and critical thinking, and to compare their own works with those of the early artists through field trips to local museums where collections of works are on display.

I emphasize the relationship of history to art and vice versa, but the well-rounded visual arts program also helps students reinforce and sharpen their skills and knowledge in language arts, mathematics, science, and other of the social studies. For example, by studying calligraphy, students might improve their abilities in math and spelling; by studying linear perspective and patterns, their knowledge of math and urban environment. Whatever your approach, the goal should be to give students the chance to study and learn from various visual art forms, for these art forms contain the highest aspirations of the human spirit. (Rosina Lopez de Short)

These are the comments received about the preceding statement.

Darlene Frazier, art department chair, Boone (Iowa) Junior-Senior High School

I encourage educators to look beyond the basics in viewing the value of art education. Important as basic subjects may be, they fulfill only a part of students' needs in the learning process. Students look not only for relevancy in their studies, but also for diversity. We must respect this if we want them to continue educational pursuits both in and out of school.

Reprinted from *Today's Education*, 1984-85 Annual Edition. © 1984 by the National Education Association.

Art experiences provide evidence of the thinking process. Art is, after all, a form of communication, and it must be recognized as such. Basics help us live. Going beyond basics makes living worthwhile!

Aldona Downing, art teacher, West Willington (Connecticut) Center School

Appreciating other cultures begins with appreciating your own. Rosina Short's approach to teaching visual arts by using native forms, procedures, and materials seems to confirm this. Very often we lose sight of our own culture by stressing others.

For example, although the Statue of Liberty is a symbol to people who want to escape tyranny, it first symbolizes American democratic principles.

By stressing authenticity among her students, even though two-dimensional drawing may be the result, Short is teaching a lesson we all may profit from: authenticity is more important than technique.

Paul D. Hayes, art teacher, Laurel (Delaware) Middle School

I agree that art is a vital part of a student's education. Drawing for example, shouldn't be left to the once-a-week art lesson. The ability to perceive and accurately render the three-dimensional world on a two-dimensional surface is an important ''basic'' skill that students should study and practice daily. Drawing stimulates and develops the right—or spatial—hemisphere of the brain, the hemisphere responsible for creative thinking in any discipline. Drawing is a simple, overlooked avenue for the planned, assured development of spatial perception and manipulation, which are basic skills.

MUSIC AND THEATER EDUCATION

Are the arts in danger? Will education reforms that require more hours in nonelective courses prove the undoing of school arts programs? Wright State University fine arts educator Sharon Rasor, whose specialty is music, and Rita Kotter, a 25-year theater teaching veteran who now heads the Fine Arts Center at Fairview High in Boulder, Colorado, believe arts programs must be considered essential parts of the school curriculum. How can schools make the arts come alive? Rasor and Kotter offer several different prescriptions.

Music Education

Music has been a means of expression and a touchstone for sensitivity throughout human existence. Through music and the other arts, our senses become more acute, our minds more alert, and our creative expression nurtured. The development and growth of these human abilities is essential for perpetuating a society of compassion and intellectual vitality.

Currently, our schools' emphasis on academic excellence defined in terms of high technology threatens quality music education—and all quality arts education. How can we provide music instruction which fosters students' intellectual, emotional, and social growth? Here are some ideas.

— Insist that thoroughly trained and skilled music specialists be employed. With their aid, students can learn to read music, to hear and understand the elements of music—such as melody, rhythm, and harmony—and to use this knowledge in performance and other creative pursuits.

— Provide opportunities for musical performances that grow out of music instruction, demonstrating the students' musical development.

— Explore with the students the use of music for human expression in earlier times, in various cultures, and in our society.

— Listen carefully to students' observations on music to gain a better understanding of their interaction with it.

— Develop good communication among the administrators and the teaching staff so they can exchange knowledge and ideas.

Music instruction plays an important part in the education of our students. With the help of school administrators who are sensitive to the value of arts in our society, it will continue to do so. (Sharon Rasor)

The two responses were:

Kate Drew, elementary teacher, Ainsworth School, Portland, Oregon

I applaud Sharon Rasor's article. Our entire culture flourishes when our arts are nurtured. We are diminished when school and taxing authorities fail to grasp the importance of arts education for total educational excellence.

Music is a highly specialized area, requiring skills beyond the academic disciplines in which most teachers are trained. Many teachers do incorporate music into their programs, cooperating with music specialists to produce exciting results. At Ainsworth School, music traditionally has been valued and so has been an integral part of our program.

Lois Ulvin, elementary music supervisor, School District of Beloit, Wisconsin

We as music educators must always be accountable for our programs and ready to provide facts about the impact of our teaching on each child's education and preparation for life.

The results of music education may seem intangible, but numerous reports indicate that study of the arts develops learning skills necessary in other disciplines. The teaching of music and the arts in our schools ensures the education of the total child and makes for the harmonious world we all wish to live in.

49

GARDNER WEBB COLLEGE LIBRARY

Theater Education

People often ask me what happens in my theater classroom: just what skills and content do I teach, and by what means?

The content I teach is dramatic literature as it mirrors culture, politics, customs and universal human needs and motivations. In studying each play, we ask: What was happening in that period? How are those characters like me or someone I know?

Theater skills involve both thinking and expression. Students analyze plot structure, delineate character, recognize theme and purpose, understand current issues. They read aloud, discuss, research background, and write. They try out ways to interpret a character from printed page to live performance. Evaluation of the final production, guided by the teacher, helps them recognize which techniques worked and why.

Theater education is not just for future career theater artists; it also prepares discriminating and responsive audience members who can find new meaning in their lives by sharing the experiences of others.

A trained theater teacher backed by the administration offers excellence in education, yet the field's importance is not always acknowledged. We as theater teachers can take action to secure the proper support for theater education by marking the arts sections of recent education reports and giving copies to parents, administrators, and school board members. We can also report to these people about our classes' work and invite them to share in classes and productions. (Rita Kotter)

Judith Rethwisch, speech and dramatics chair, Affton High School, St. Louis, Missouri commented:

I concur with Rita Kotter's assessment of the arts in education today. I teach the same skills of communication in English as in dramatics/speech. But one course is considered an essential; the other, "just an elective."

The growth of the electronic media has given the edge to people who can think rationally and critically and can persuade, convince, and motivate others. These techniques are the very skills taught in speech/drama classes, and it is these skills that students use daily to compete.

Resources

The following materials are recommended as useful to visual arts, music, and theater educators, in conjunction with this chapter.

Visual Arts

Art, Culture, and Environment: A Catalyst for Teaching. June K. McFee and Rogena M. Degge, Kendall-Hunt, 1980.

Art is Elementary: Teaching Visual Thinking Through Art Concepts. Iva M. Cornia, et al. Brigham Young University Press, 1976.

Developing Artistic and Perceptual Awareness: Art Practice in the Elementary Classroom. Earl Linderman and Donald Herbholz. William C. Brown, 1979.

Drawing on the Right Side of the Brain. Betty Edwards. J. P. Tarcher, 1979.

Hispanic Arts and Ethnohistory in the Southwest: New Papers Inspired by the Work of E. Boyd. Marta Weigle and Claudia Larcombe (eds.). Ancient City Press, 1983.

New Mexico Village Arts. Ronald F. Dickey. University of New Mexico Press, 1970.

Music

Bowmar Orchestral Library. (Recordings.) Bowmar/Noble Publishers.

Higher Education and the Arts in the United States. National Association of Schools of Music, 1984.

The Music Book. Holt, Rinehart and Winston, 1981.

The Spectrum of Music. Macmillan, 1974.

Teaching Music. James P. O'Brien, Holt, Rinehart and Winston, 1983.

Theater

Acting, the Creative Process. Hardie and Arnita Albright. Wadsworth Pub. Co., 1980.

Great Scenes from the World Theatre. James L. Steffensen, Jr., ed. Avon, vol. 1, 1965; vol. 2, 1972.

The Stage and the School. Katharine Ommanney and Harry Schanker. Fifth edition. McGraw-Hill, 1982.

Stage Crafts. Chris Hoggett. St. Martin's Press, 1977.

Chapter 13

THE COMPUTER IN THE FINE ARTS: VISUAL ARTS, MUSIC, THEATER

Henry S. Kepner, Jr.

Often the computer is considered a piece of technology that should be classified with the physical sciences and mathematics. Its capabilities to serve as a tool for creative human thought cannot be limited to this narrow field, however. Furthermore, the low cost and accessibility of microcomputers have made them tools of the fine arts in schools, not just in isolated institutes.

In this brief review it is not possible to explore the multitude of existing and potential applications of the computer for arts educators and their students. Rather, the following examples are intended to encourage enthusiasm among teachers to explore the huge possibilities the computer offers. Across the country dramatic and exciting computer projects are now in place in the arts curricula, in elementary, middle, and secondary schools. The focus here is on the visual arts, music, and theater.

VISUAL ARTS

Once again, with the advent of new materials and creative individuals who use them for expression, the definition of art is expanding. Computer graphics is the new medium of this expression. Examples are available daily through television. Cartoon shows—especially the Saturday morning series—and commericals include animation generated through computer graphics. Most big-league sports arenas have large display boards that are computer-controlled. These changeable message boards are becoming highly popular atop buildings and on billboards.

There are two distinct methods of generating a computer image for transfer to paper, TV monitor, or electronic sign. In the first method, referred to as the "digitized image," and "image is provided as data to the computer [which is] external to a computer program" (5, p. 45). In this method, someone plans out the representation on a grid which corresponds to the number of dots or lattice points on the video screen or sign. Thus, the form is first sketched on paper and then translated to computer data for reproduction on the monitor. The first inexpensive microcomputer to give students the opportunity to graph easily in color is the Apple II computer.

Students can choose a 16-color low resolution display with a 40 × 40 matrix or an 8-color 280 horizontal × 193 vertical high-resolution display. The author has worked with third graders who have generated an untold number of images by plotting out their picture using the 40 × 40 or 280 × 193 array. These students have created words, lettering, maps, and such favorite friends as Snoopy and the Hulk.

The second method of generating a computer image uses algorithms or procedures which are part of a computer program. An early procedure studied by elementary school students is random art. Using the computer's random number generator, students program the computer to randomly select a point on the screen and an available color or character. These images are projected on the screen at a rapid rate. Since the background "color" on the screen is a color choice, the user notices that points disappear. A run of this program fascinates both children and adults.

The grid structure of the display unit forces computer graphics to be mathematical in nature. Thus, work with equations of known figures—lines, circles, sine curves—is helpful in gaining mastery of the potential of computer art. One form of art "is distinguished by the fact that it is precisely the equations themselves which give the figures beauty and appeal" (8, p. 105). Numerous examples of art based on equations of curves, polynomial functions, and periodic functions (sine, cosine) are widely displayed in the art world (14).

Students do not have to know mathematical equations to develop a curve, sketch, or cartoon character. Several companies have developed graphics tablets on which figures may be drawn with an electronic pen. This electronic board transfers the image to computer memory. The electronically stored information can then be represented on the video monitor or on paper.

Using the mathematics of movement in the plane of three-dimensional space, students have been extending the work with Escher-like art (5, p. 49). This movement allows designers to build a graphics model of an object and then rotate it to see it, in perspective, from any

Adapted from *Computers in the Classroom*. © 1982 by the National Education Association.

point of view. The procedure is common practice in architecture, aircraft and auto design, and also in tool and die design. More recently, chemists have been using this design method in creating potential molecular structures such as DNA-type chains.

The field of graphics communication has also moved to computer-based artwork and production. An entire issue of *U & lc* (Upper and Lower Case), the international journal of typographics, was devoted to acquainting practitioners with the new technology and its functions (11). The opening editorial of a later issue set the focus: "New kinds of typesetters and electronic page makeup devices, graphic creation stations and display terminals, even the electronic/digital typesetting of color halftones, are commercial realities." (12, p.3). Thus a major concern of the graphics communication profession is the adequate training of entering students in computer uses.

Computers and display units are now available at reasonable cost for the study and construction of visual representation. They allow the introduction of movement to previously static art forms. Students are already exploring these capabilities in the school setting. Since the art is generated by a computer progam and associated data, the expense of the art form is relatively cheap. And the computer can be used over and over again—it is not a consumable supply.

MUSIC

To the surprise of many people, the computer is opening a whole new accessibility to music for adults, students, and the school curriculum. Existing computer programs allow the user to compose music for up to 16 voices, play music entered in the computer, display notes on a video screen, edit existing music, and hear music through stereo amplifiers (6).

Electronic music has been in existence for nearly half a century. Now, a special form has come into its own— computer music. According to Kitsz, "Computer music is fully electronic sound in which the actual waveforms, envelope (electronic equivalent of an embouchure), volume and so on have been calculated and created by a computer under the composer's direction." (4, p. 27).

For instructional uses, several companies and individuals have developed curriculum packages that provide computer-assisted drills. The drills are usually intended for individual student work following classroom instruction. Programs currently in use drill on these topics: stating interval distance, writing or identifying scales, recognizing rhythm patterns, recognizing whole- and half-steps, identifying which note shown on the screen was not played, identifying which note in an observed phrase was played wrongly, and stating the type of triad played. These drills permit individual response to the correspondence between sheet music and the music heard. They are a major extension of the group response to a record or to a teacher at the piano for individual students. They greatly enhance the opportunities for learning

how to read sheet music and to recognize patterns, especially for nonperforming students. Most of these programs are available for the Apple II, as well as other computers.

Clark, et al. provide another drill example of computer-aided sightreading (2). They describe and list a program that generates 10 random notes on the staff following the students' choice of clef. The program, written for the TRS-80, Level II, 16K RAM memory, times the student's attempts to sightread using keys labelled DO, RE, etc.

For many students, the opportunity to compose music through the computer opens a new area of exploration. As a nonperformer, the author has thrilled at composing a short score and hearing it played, and after each playing has made modifications to improve the quality. On a small scale, this experience parallels that of most composers as they hear a composition performed for the first time. For example, on the television special honoring his eightieth birthday (aired in November 1980), Aaron Copland noted: "The ecstasy of hearing a piece you composed for the first time. You think you know what it was like, but you're never really sure!"

In music appreciation, the example of a theme is presented frequently, but it is often difficult for the untrained ear to pick up a repeated segment by listening to a full orchestral performance on record or tape. When segments of such a piece are stored in a computer, teachers have control over which parts, or voices, to play. They can play a segment repeatedly, each time adding or deleting other voices so that students can follow a major or minor thread in the score.

For the musician, the computer is a new instrument to be challenged—one that tirelessly plays what the composer writes, modifies, and embellishes. For the educator, the computer is an instructional tool that provides individual drill on music fundamentals and appreciation skills, even for the nonperformer. For the nonperformer, the computer presents an opportunity to be involved in music construction.

Certainly, the collection of educational activities in music is unfinished.

THEATER

For the theater, the major uses of the computer focus on management and script and stagecraft directions. The computer is an ideal tool for listing the inventory of company sets, costumes, props, lights, and the like. On the other hand, the computer as a word processor is ideal for making changes in scripts, stage directions, and lighting sequences. These changes can be made electronically without the need to retype the entire copy manually.

In recent professional performances, for example, computer-controlled lights were needed to provide the intended effect. Frequent, complex lighting changes could not have been made manually with the required precision. Although such electronics are not available for school theater performances at this time, the basic electronic units may be within budget limitations in the future.

References

1. Borry, L. "Meet the Music Teacher's New Assistant—A Microcomputer." *AEDS Monitor* (October–December 1979): 21.

2. Clark, D. B.; Wilkins, C. T.; and Tuma, D. T. "Computer-Aided Sightreading." *Creative Computing* 6, no. 6 (June 1980): 84–88.

3. Ettinger, L., and Rayala, M. "Computers in Art Education." *Computing Teacher* 8, no. 4 (1980–81): 24–29.

4. Kitsz, D. "A Short History of Computer Music." *Microcomputing* (December 1980): 27–30.

5. Kolomyjec, W. J. "The Appeal of Computer Graphics." In *Artist and Computer*, edited by R. Leavitt. Morristown, N.J.: Creative Computing Press, 1976.

6. Mercuri, R. T. "Music Editors for Small Computers." *Creative Computing* 7, no. 2 (February 1981): 18–24.

7. Micro Music, Inc. 213 Cambridge Dr., P.O. Box 386, Normal, IL 61761.

8. Schmucker, K. "The Mathematics of Computer Art." *Byte* 4, no. 7 (July 1979): 105–116.

9. Tubb, P. "Apple Music Synthesizer." *Creative Computing* 6, no. 6 (June 1980): 74–83.

10. _____. "Musical Subroutines." *Creative Computing* 8, no. 3 (March 1982): 124–32.

11. *U & lc* 7, no. 2 (June 1980).

12. _____ 7, no. 4 (December 1980).

13. Waite, M. *Computer Graphics Primer*. Indianapolis: Howard W. Sams and Co., 1979.

14. Walter, R. "Creating Computer Art." *Creative Computing* 4, no. 3 (May–June 1978): 84–86.

Chapter 14

ROBERT'S PROBLEM . . . OR OURS? VISUALS IN THE CLASSROOM

Frederick B. Tuttle, Jr.

I recently read an article which presented a human interest story about Robert, a near failure in high school because he could not read the required materials. Assuming that all of Robert's problems resulted from his poor reading skills, the author concluded that the school should revise its curricula to teach Robert these necessary skills. This change would necessitate one of several alternatives: supplementing Robert's academic program with independent work on reading skills; giving him an extra class in remedial reading while he was carrying a full academic load; or grouping him with other poor readers in order to concentrate on his reading skills without concern for the more academic work. On the surface these efforts appear to be for Robert's benefit. However, they actually may work against Robert. The first two suggestions would place an extra burden on a student who already has considerable difficulty supporting his academic load. The third program would relegate Robert to an academically second-rate future. Even if he did improve his reading skills in this third program, he would probably have to remain in the "C-group" because he would not have had the academic preparation of the "regular groups." Consequently, just to catch up with these students, Robert would have to do extra work. While this is difficult enough for one who has confidence in himself, it is nearly impossible for one who has been branded a failure by both the school and himself.

Other conclusions to this anecdote are possible, however. Perhaps the problem is not only Robert's inability to read the textbooks, but also the teachers' inabilities to deal with concepts and ideas without requiring strong reading skills. What is really important? Four hundred thirty-two printed words or the feelings of repression the colonists felt prior to the American Revolution? A three page critical analysis of a poem or the student's reactions to the message, images, and insights of the poem? Ideally, it is the latter, the concepts, reactions and feelings. Actually, in many schools it is the former, the printed word. Most lessons which teachers consider important are based on a reading assignment.

"Read chapter twelve in the text for discussion tomorrow." To insure the students' reading of the assignment, teachers sometimes give a short quiz at the beginning of the next class. Even without a formal quiz the class is usually a test situation, as most discussion questions refer directly to the assigned reading. The conscientious student who has difficulty reading and, therefore, is unable to read chapter twelve, is severely punished twice, possibly thrice. First, he spends an emotionally and intellectually frustrating hour or so struggling with chapter twelve—feeling less and less adequate to cope with this world of academia with each passing line of print. Second, he fails the short quiz or the full-class "test," thereby confirming the teacher's belief that he is lazy or just "dumb," adding another failure to his intellectual record. Third, and least acknowledged, this student wastes another forty-five minutes in class because he is unable to participate in the lesson. One more day into the semester; one more day wasted; and one more day further behind all the "readers."

What is the cause? Authoritarian, insensitive teachers? No. Many democratic, sensitive teachers also face "Roberts" every day and find themselves unable to bring them into the class. Is it Robert's lack of reading skills? Partially, at least under the present mode of academic communication. Or is it the teachers' inability to communicate concepts through media other than print? Probably. it is true many teachers use films, role situations, large and small group discussions, and so on; but it is also true that many of these teachers base the "important" lessons on the reading and treat the other situations as introductory, supplementary, or just fun.

For most teachers the "real meat" of a lesson is the print rather than the concept which is being communicated. The concept is not the printed word. It is the feelings, the ideas, and questions raised by the medium through which it is communicated. While in most academic situations the chosen medium is print, for effective communication the message should be communicated. A concept, however, is a message which should be communicated through the most appropriate medium for both sender (teacher) and, especially, receiver (student). In some cases this may be print. In many other cases, however, it is a medium other than print. Thus, the prob-

Reprinted with permission from *Connecticut English Journal*, Fall 1978.

lem is not necessarily the student's lack of reading skills, but rather the teachers' inability to communicate concepts through a variety of methods and media.

Is there a solution? Yes. Magazines such as *Media and Methods* and *Learning* have been demonstrating a variety of possible solutions for years; but before these methods can be implemented effectively, there has to be a change of attitude. The use of more media and a wider variety of teaching methods is the outward effect of what should be an inner change of attitude toward teaching. First, the teacher has to admit that reading is only one method of arriving at the understanding of a concept. Too many of us treat the printed word as the concept itself rather than as a tool to implement understanding. Then, each teacher has to examine his/her own curriculum to determine the concepts (not the chapters) he/she wants to teach. This re-examination may be shockingly revealing to many. The teacher may, for example, find that some of what has been taught merely because it is in the text is actually irrelevant to both the course goals and to the students' needs.

Once the concepts are delineated, the teacher begins a search for a variety of media and methods to communicate them. Print may be one of the media and silent reading may be one of the methods; but certainly, as has been aptly demonstrated by creative teachers, there are many other media and methods through which concepts can be more effectively examined by each student in the class, especially by the "Roberts." For example, in teaching the concept of division of labor, the teacher might have the class live the experience through simulation. To do this the class could be divided into two groups; one which would produce model cars in an assembly line fashion and one which would make them individually. After a specified length of time, the groups could discuss the two methods in terms of amount of output, ease of production, quality of work, and feelings of individuals during production. In this way the class would deal with the concept without having to rely on chapter twelve of the text.

This approach would help the poor readers understand the ideas the teacher is presenting, but how will the teacher know that students do, in fact, understand the concept? Teachers usually determine comprehension by giving a test or having students write essays to explain their understanding. If students, however, have difficulty reading, it is safe to assume they also have considerable difficulty taking a test or writing. Consequently, the teacher should allow students opportunities to demonstrate their comprehension of the ideas through media other than print. For example, a student might give a reaction to a poem through a slide-tape interpretation of the ideas rather than write a three page analytical essay. Just as print is only one form of sending a message, it is also only one of many ways for the teacher to receive feedback from the student.

Does this mean that reading skills should not be taught? No. In fact, each content teacher should examine the type of reading the course requires and then teach these specific reading skills, again through a variety of techniques and media. In English, for example, determining point of view is an important reading skill. This is often taught by having students read a passage and then determine the speaker, defending their choices with clues from the passage. If a student has difficulty reading the passage, he/she will probably not be able to take part in the lesson and will, therefore, not learn point of view. An alternative method of teaching this concept would be to examine point of view as used in a film. By discussing the film with questions such as "through whose eyes do we see the world?" we can stress the various clues which help determine point of view. This skill, once learned and discussed with a film, would then be transferred to a reading situation, constantly referring back to similar clues found in the film.

Using media other than print has an additional benefit for poor readers. Since much of their reading problem is non-use rather than a lack of comprehension skills, this kind of approach to teaching skills and concepts should help poor readers overcome some of their reading problems. First, it often allows students who have failed in most of their classes to be successful in an academic setting. They, as well as the honor students, can see the film. Once their self-confidence is bolstered enough to let them respond on an equal footing with other students, they might be more willing to try these skills with their reading. Second, while this approach helps poor readers use their comprehension skills more actively and successfully in academic situations, it also provides them with the conceptual background necessary for understanding the printed versions of similar ideas. Consequently, if we can show students how to apply comprehension skills in one medium, we may be able to help them transfer this knowledge and confidence to print.

In sum, teachers do have an obligation to teach reading skills; but first we have an obligation to teach concepts. If we look closely at the concepts we teach, we should be able to find ways to allow the "Roberts" to understand and to take an active role in class while they are also increasing their reading skills. Otherwise, they will never have an equal chance to achieve academic equality. They will be segregated from others on the basis of a deficiency in one area—reading.

Chapter 15

THE IMPLICATIONS FOR THE ARTS OF RECENT EDUCATION STUDIES AND REPORTS

Charles B. Fowler

The arts community has great stakes in the educational debates that undoubtedly will result from the publication and wide distribution of a marathon of publicly and privately commissioned educational studies and reports. Several of these reports have already been published; more are on the way. So far, all of the studies have focused on the public schools. The reports, which vary in length from 20 to upwards of 400 pages are highly critical and offer a wide range of proposed solutions. The place of the arts in these new curricular proposals varies from one report to the next.

What follows is an analysis of what exactly these reports say about the arts and their implications for arts education.

DISCREPANCIES

The Importance of the Arts

While these reports are fairly consistent about the importance of English, mathematics, science, and other "academic" subjects, they present widely conflicting and confusing accounts for the arts and their value and place in American schools. For example: Those who support arts education can take considerable satisfaction from four of the reports that express varying degrees of support for the arts ranging from a generous nod to declaring them one of the basic, or part of the "core" of learning. But at the same time, two of the reports—one by the Twentieth Century Fund, the other by the Education Commission of the States—do not mention the arts at all. Given the fact that these studies uphold the importance of other subject matters such as science and mathematics, one can infer that they are not supportive of the arts.

How Academic?

Taken together, there are also confusions in these reports concerning how academic the arts should be. The College Board views them as largely academic. It recommends that college entrants develop knowledge and skills "in at least one art form" that cover the broad range of history, theory, criticism, and performance. The National Commission recommends that the arts require "rigorous effort" and that "they should demand the same level of performance as the Basics." The Education Commission of the States recommends that schools "eliminate 'soft' non-essential courses," implying, one can surmise, that if the arts are to remain, they must be taught as academic disciplines.

There seems to be consistent agreement here that the arts should become more academic. But, oddly enough, Goodlad found in his observations of arts classes at all levels that one of their worst qualities was apparent precisely when they emulated the so-called academic subjects. He says:

> I am disappointed with the degree to which arts classes appear to be dominated by the ambience of English, mathematics, and other academic subjects. Arts classes, too, appear to be governed by characteristics which are best described as "school"—following the rules, finding the one right answer, practicing the lower cognitive processes.[1]

In which direction, then, should the arts move—toward an academic profile similar to other subjects or toward capitalizing more successfully upon their indigenous individuality? This question, undoubtedly, will be one of the issues of the 80's.

Reprinted with permission from *Arts in Education/Education in Arts: Entering Dialogue of the 80's*, National Endowment for the Arts in Education, 1984.

Focus and Depth

In his study of the high school, Ernest Boyer values the arts because they "give expression to the profound urgings of the human spirit . . . " He says that, if we are to survive together, "Now, more than ever all people need to see clearly, hear acutely, and feel sensitively through the arts."[2]

But again, Goodlad, in a second reservation regarding the conduct of arts programs in the schools, observes that these programs do not live up to their highest possibilities. He says:

> There was a noticeable absence of emphasis on the arts as cultural expression and artifact. The need for expression lies just back of the human need for food, water, and socialization. Yet the impression I get of the arts programs in the schools studied is that they go little beyond coloring, polishing, and playing—and much of this goes on in classes such as social studies as a kind of auxiliary activity rather than as art in its own right. What does not come through in our data is much if any indication that the arts were being perceived as central to personal satisfaction in a world rich in art forms, processes and products. To grow up without the opportunity to develop such sophistication in arts appreciation is to grow up deprived.[3]

Apparently, the focus and depth of arts education programs are a matter that needs some study and resolution.

Self-Expression/Creativity

Goodlad also found that arts classes "did not convey the picture of individual expression and artistic creativity toward which one is led by the rhetoric of forward-looking practice in the field."[4] He indicts the arts for not living up to their expressed purposes and goals. In other words, arts education justifies its value in education on the basis of its importance to self-expression and creativity (among other qualities), but it doesn't deliver on those promises. This, too, could become an issue in the 80's.

The matter of creativity is an important consideration in these reports. Most of these studies enlist education in the economic battle to keep America competitive in global markets. For example, *A Nation at Risk* states that "Our once unchallenged preeminence in commerce, industry, science, and technological *innovation* is being overtaken by competitors throughout the world." The Education Commission of the States declares that "our faith in ourselves as the world's supreme *innovators*—is being shaken." Increasingly, this task force says, jobs that offer upward mobility will be "those which require the *creative* use of technology." [Emphasis mine]

Yet with so much expressed concern in these reports for the development of innovation and creativity, it is ironical that they do not make the obvious connection

to the arts. (Perhaps it is because, as Goodlad points out, arts education doesn't make that connection in its own practice.) It is doubtful whether this nation can remain the world's leader in technological inventiveness without investing in the creative development of its young minds. It seems short-sighted to want to remain competitive in this technological world yet not realize that the arts encourage people to be innovative and to value their creative selves. In this sense, some of these reports seriously underestimate the educational potential of the arts. After all, students don't learn to be creative in spelling, math, or history.

College Admission Policies

The reports disagree in another important area—whether the arts should be considered important for college entrance. The College Board views the arts as "valuable" to college students "whatever their intended field of study," a marked turnabout for an organization that has long maintained testing for college admission based upon scores in verbal and mathematical aptitude.

In contrast, the National Commission's report states that:

> Four-year colleges and universities should raise their admissions requirements and advise all potential applicants of the standards for admissions in terms of specific courses, performance in these areas, and levels of achievement on standardized achievement tests in each of the five Basics [English, mathematics, science, social studies, and computer science] and, where applicable, foreign languages.[5]

The arts are not included. We know from long experience that high schools teach what is tested. Achievement tests are prescriptive; they determine curricula. They tell students and teachers what is important and what is not. By *not* counting the arts important for college entrance, the Commission consigns them, deliberately or inadvertently, to an inferior status.

CONFUSING MESSAGES

I submit that these reports are sending confusing signals to the American public, to state legislators to school boards, to administrators and teachers, and to educational organizations regarding the role and value of the arts in education. Depending upon which reports gain prominence, the arts could become central to education or be even further relegated to the educational sidelines.

The point is: These same studies are *not* sending confusing signals about English, math, science, social studies, even foreign languages and computer science. Necessarily, the arts education profession is left to ponder the questions: What might be sacrificed in the rush to produce more scientists and mathematicians? In our haste to make curricular changes, will we forget that there are lots of different kinds of kids out there? What kinds of opportunities for learning truly enable children to develop their fullest potential?

As the state and local debates on educational reform warm up in the coming months, arts supporters will want to be armed with what these reports say about the arts in order to enter these important dialogues with some authority. The national priority now being given to education is an opportunity for major improvements. The discussions, planning, and, ultimately, the changes that these reports will generate command informed participation by the arts community.

What follows, then, are highlights on the arts and other related material from these important new studies.

ANALYSES

I

A Nation At Risk: The Imperative for Educational Reform. Report of the National Commission on Excellence in Education (Washington, D.C.: U.S. Government Printing Office, 1983).

This report is the result of a study initiated by the Secretary of Education of the U.S. Department of Education and is issued as an open letter to the American people. These recommendations have commanded high visibility in the media, but what the report states about the arts has been largely ignored.

The report announces that "Our once unchallenged preeminence in commerce, industry, science, and technological innovation is being overtaken by competitors throughout the world." It recommends that we must reform our educational system "if only to keep and improve on the slim competitive edge we still retain in world markets . . . ." It mobilizes education to solve America's international problems of industry and commerce in much the same way that we marshaled education in the years following Russia's Sputnik to regain our worldwide lead in science and technology.

But, the Commission states, its concerns go "well beyond matters such as industry and commerce," and include "the intellectual, moral, and spiritual strengths of our people which knit together the very fabric of our society." Even more important, in terms of the arts, the report states that "educational reform should focus on the goal of creating a Learning Society"—that education is important not only for practical purposes "but also because of the value it adds to the general quality of one's life." The Commission views museums and other cultural institutions as important resources that "offer opportunities and choices for all to learn throughout life."

The problem of balance in the curriculum is faced forthrightly. The report acknowledges that people "are concerned that an over-emphasis on technical and occupational skills will leave little time for studying the arts and humanities that so enrich daily life, help maintain civility, and develop a sense of community." It maintains that knowledge of the humanities [including the arts] "must be harnessed to science and technology if the latter are to remain creative and humane, just as the humanities need to be informed by science and technology if they are to remain relevant to the human condition."

While the Commission recommends a curriculum comprised for "Five New Basics"—English, mathematics, sciences, social studies, and computer science—it further states that "A high level of shared education in these Basics, together with work in the fine and performing arts and foreign languages, constitutes the mind and spirit of our culture."

"In addition to the New Basics," the report declares, "other important curriculum matters must be addressed." Here the report recommends "rigorous effort in subjects that advance students' personal, educational, and occupational goals, such as the fine and performing arts . . . "—areas that "complement the New Basics."

The arts are also specifically mentioned as one of the areas in which students should be provided a "sound base" during the eight grades leading to the high school years. "These years," the report says, "should foster an enthusiasm for learning and the development of the individual's gifts and talents."

The report indicates that teaching in the arts has suffered from the same problems as teaching in all subjects, and recommends that they should be taught more rigorously than at present. The arts, the Commission says, "should demand the same level of performance as the Basics."

Among the recommendations, the Commission calls for "more effective use of the existing school day, a longer school day, or a lengthened school year." It also recommends that high school students "be assigned far more homework than is now the case." Other recommendations deal with improving teaching, leadership, and fiscal support, areas that would help the arts as much as any subject.

In a concluding section, the report asks parents "to nurture your child's curiosity, creativity, and confidence;" and, while it doesn't specify *how*, a strong case could be made that these qualities can best be developed by involvement with one or more of the arts.

"A Final Word" at the end of the report makes a plea for "all segments of our population" to give attention "to the implementation of our recommendations."

Our present plight did not appear overnight, and the responsibility for our current situation is widespread. Reform of our educational system will take time and unwavering commitment. It will require equally widespread, energetic, and dedicated action.

The report then calls upon specific agencies, including the "National Endowment for the Humanities, National Endowment for the Arts, and other scholarly, scientific and learned societies for their help in this effort."

The report ends with a statement of mission:

It is by our willingness to take up the challenge, and our resolve to see it through, that America's place in the world will be either secured or forfeited. Americans have succeeded before and so we shall again.

II

Academic Preparation for College: What Students Need to Know and Be Able to Do. Report of the Educational EQuality Project of the College Entrance Examination Board (New York: College Board Publications, 1983).

The Educational EQuality* Project of the College Entrance Examination Board has issued this report as part of a ten-year effort to strengthen the academic quality of secondary education. The report proposes a core curriculum comprised of six "basic academic subjects"—English, mathematics, science, social studies, foreign languages, and the arts.

The report details why students preparing for college need these subjects and specifies the skills they should learn in each area. In explaining why the arts are needed, for example, the report states that they "challenge and extend human experience," represent "a unique record of diverse cultures," and "provide distinctive ways of understanding human beings and nature."

The arts are valued as "creative modes by which all people can enrich their lives both by self-expression and response to the expressions of others." Works of art are viewed as "complex systems of expression" requiring "careful reasoning and sustained study that lead to informed insight." Just as a thorough understanding of science necessitates laboratory or field work, understanding the arts requires "first-hand work in them."

The report recognizes that such high school preparation in the arts will enable college students to engage in and profit from advanced study that, for some, will lead to careers in the arts. But it also acknowledges that, for many others, such study "will permanently enhance the quality of their lives, whether they continue artistic activity as an avocation or appreciation of the arts as observers and members of audiences." The report views the arts as "valuable" to college students "whatever their intended field of study" because they "engage the imagination, foster flexible ways of thinking, develop disciplined effort, and build self-confidence."

The report states that college-bound students should have the following background in the arts:

- The ability to understand and appreciate the unique qualities of each of the arts.
- The ability to appreciate how people of various cultures have used the arts to express themselves.
- The ability to understand and appreciate different artistic styles and works from representative historical periods and cultures.
- Some knowledge of the social and intellectual influences affecting artistic form.
- The ability to use the skills, media, tools, and processes required to express themselves in one or more of the arts.

The report further suggests "intensive preparation" in at least one art form, and it lists in detail specific knowledge and skills college entrants will need in visual arts, theater, music, and dance that cover the broad range of history, theory, criticism, and performance:

If the preparation of college entrants is in the *visual arts*, they will need the following knowledge and skills.

- The ability to identify and describe—using the appropriate vocabulary—various visual art forms from different historical periods.
- The ability to analyze the structure of a work of visual art.
- The ability to evaluate a work of visual art.
- To know how to express themselves in one or more of the visual art forms, such as drawing, painting, photography, weaving, ceramics, and sculpture.

If the preparation of college entrants is in *theater*, they will need the following knowledge and skills.

- The ability to identify and describe—using the appropriate vocabulary—different kinds of plays from different historical periods.
- The ability to analyze the structure, plot, characterization, and language of a play, both as a literary document and as a theater production.
- The ability to evaluate a theater production.
- To know how to express themselves by acting in a play or by improvising, or by writing a play, or by directing or working behind the scenes of a theater production.

If the preparation of college entrants is in *music*, they will need the following knowledge and skills.

- The ability to identify and describe—using the appropriate vocabulary—various musical forms from different historical periods.
- The ability to listen perceptively to music, distinguishing such elements as pitch, rhythm, timbre, and dynamics.

---

*Both the "E" and "Q" are capitalized to indicate the project's intertwined emphases on Quality and Equality.

- The ability to read music.
- The ability to evaluate a musical work or performance.
- To know how to express themselves by playing an instrument, singing in a group or individually, or composing music.

If the preparation of college entrants is in *dance*, they will need the following knowledge and skills.

- The ability to identify and describe—using the appropriate vocabulary—dances of various cultures and historical periods.
- The ability to analyze various techniques, styles, and choreographic forms.
- The ability to evaluate a dance performance.
- To know how to express themselves through dancing or choreography.[6]

Even though this report does not attempt to suggest curricula for students who do not choose to prepare for college, it states that "much of the learning described here also can be valuable to students going directly into the world of work." Such in-depth high school courses in the arts imply that the foundation for this study is to be provided in elementary and junior high schools, as the report makes clear: "Improving preparation for college will also involve strengthening elementary and junior high school curricula."

III

Ernest L. Boyer. *High School: A Report on Secondary Education in America*, by The Carnegie Foundation for the Advancement of Teaching (New York: Harper & Row, Publishers, 1983).

After two-and-a-half years of study that involved 2,000 hours of observations and interviews in high schools across the country, this report concludes that "the academic report card on the nation's schools is mixed." Here is the way the report evaluates high schools today:

For a small percentage of students—10 to 15 percent perhaps—the American high school provides an outstanding education, the finest in the world. Their schooling combines a solid curriculum with good teaching. Students not only are expected to remember and recite, but also to explore, to think creatively, and to challenge. A larger percentage of students— perhaps 20 to 30 percent—mark time in school or drop out. For them, the high school experience occasionally may be socially supportive, but academically it's a failure. The majority of students are in the vast middle ground. . . . They attend high schools that, like the communities that surround them, are surviving but not thriving.

The report proposes 12 key strategies for school reform ranging from establishing clear goals and improving the working conditions of teachers to extending the teacher's reach with technology and strengthening connections between elementary, junior, and senior high schools and between the schools, business, and industry. These themes form an agenda for action to improve secondary schools. Dozens of highly focused recommendations are included.

Within this comprehensive plan, Boyer gives four objectives top priority: the mastery of English, adopting a core curriculum with a global view, bettering the working conditions for teachers, and adding a service requirement—what is called "a new Carnegie unit"—involving volunteer work in the school or community for every high school student.

In chapter six of this 363-page report, "Literacy: The Essential Tool," Boyer states that "The first curriculum priority is language." A strong case is made here for teaching students how to write and how to speak.

The next chapter states that "The second curriculum priority is a core of common learning—a program of required courses in literature, the arts, foreign language, history, civics, science, mathematics, technology, health— to extend the knowledge and broaden the perspective of every student." The report calls for the high school curriculum to encompass a global view, stating that "American young people remain shockingly ignorant about our own heritage and about the heritage of other nations," and it recommends "that the high school help all students learn about their human heritage, and the interdependent world in which they live, through a core of common learning . . . " that moves students toward "cultural literacy."

Students, the report maintains, "should learn about the variety of ways civilization is sustained and enriched through a shared use of symbols." Here the report addresses literature and the arts, giving them top priority within the core curriculum which is "appropriate for every student—not just the college bound."

Boyer says that all students, not just the gifted, should be introduced to great literature as a means to better understand life's deeper meanings. The report states:

Literature addresses the emotional part of the human experience. It provides another perspective on historical events, telling us what matters and what has mattered to people in the past. Literature transmits from generation to generation enduring spiritual and ethical values. As an art form, literature can bring delight and re-creation. As a vehicle for illustrating moral behavior by specific examples (Job, Odysseus, Oedipus, Hamlet, Billy Budd, Captain Queeg) it speaks to all.

On the subject of the arts in general, the report could not be more supportive. It states:

From the dawn of civilization, men and women have used music, dance and the visual arts to transmit the heritage of a people and express human joys and sorrows. They are the means by which a civilization can be measured. It is not accidental that dictators, who seek to control the minds and hearts of men, suppress not just the written and spoken word, but music, dance, and the visual arts, as well. . . .

The arts are an essential part of the human experience. They are not a frill. We recommend that all students study the arts to discover how human beings use nonverbal symbols and communicate not only with words but through music, dance, and the visual arts.

The report goes on to say that "During our school visits, we found the arts to be shamefully neglected. Courses in the arts were the last to come and the first to go." Boyer maintains that "While some school districts had organized magnet schools for talented students, only one comprehensive high school we visited included art as a requirement for graduation. Nationwide, it is only rarely required."

Of those few schools that did give priority to the arts, Boyer says: "The combination of performance, experimentation, and interpretation demonstrated how exciting and rewarding the arts can be for students when they are actively involved."

Then, the rationale for support of the arts in education is given further amplification:

We conclude that the arts not only give expression to the profound urgings of the human spirit; they also validate our feelings in a world that deadens feeling. Now, more than ever, all people need to see clearly, hear acutely, and feel sensitively through the arts. These skills are no longer just desirable. They are essential if we are to survive together with civility and joy.

IV

John I. Goodlad. *A Place Called School: Prospects for the Future* (New York: McGraw-Hill Book Company, 1983).

This may be the most thorough of all the current studies of education. Goodlad and his staff of 60 spent four years studying more than 1,000 classrooms in 38 elementary and secondary schools in urban, suburban, and rural locales. Scores of questions were asked in interviews of 1,350 teachers, 8,624 parents, and 17,163 students. As a reviewer of the book stated, "One would be hard pressed to imagine a better study within the realm of reasonable human effort."

The first eight of the ten chapters present results of the research combined with Goodlad's insights gleaned from numerous other educational research studies and resources. The final two chapters offer recommendations covering the most critical problem areas. Goodlad's suggestions encompass such innovations as having children begin school at age 4 and finish at age 16, divid-

ing the 12 years of schooling into three closely linked phases of four years each; using a cluster of teachers for groups of children during each phase, utilizing more peer-group teaching, dividing large secondary schools into smaller semiautonomous units, and discontinuing the practice of tracking.

As part of his careful analysis of what goes on in schools, Goodlad provides much data of direct relevance to the arts. One of the first platitudes he shatters is that parents want schools to go "back to basics." His surveys show that people still maintain their comprehensive expectations for education. "When it comes to education," Goodlad says, "it appears that most parents want their children to have it all." By "all" he means a curriculum based on four broad areas of goals: (1) academic, (2) vocational, (3) social, civic, and cultural, and (4) personal.

He further states that commitment to this broad array of goals has "emerged in this country over more than three hundred years" and that there never was a time when the three R's were the sole expectation for schools.

Goodlad's detailed breakdown of the four goal areas presents a beginning point for discussion about what schools are for; it also provides substantiation for the importance of the arts in education. For example: under Social, Civic, and Cultural Goals, he states that students should "develop skill in communicating effectively in groups" and "develop an understanding and appreciation of cultures different from one's own." As part of the process of enculturation, students should "develop an awareness and understanding of one's cultural heritage and become familiar with the achievements of the past that have inspired and influenced humanity" and "learn how to apply the basic principles and concepts of fine arts and humanities to the appreciation of the aesthetic contributions of other cultures."

Under the area of Personal Goals, Goodlad believes that students should "develop the willingness to receive emotional impressions" and that schools should "expand one's affective sensitivity" and help students "learn to use leisure time effectively." This area includes a whole category devoted to the need to develop creativity and aesthetic expression.

Goodlad maintains that "the primary function of schools is to teach academics." At the elementary level, he says, "the school's job is an intellectual one." But he goes on to state:

With a solid academic program in place, increased attention should be given to the personal side—physical education for the body and the arts for creativity. These [parents] want it all too, but in an ordered sequence of priorities.

Observations of teaching in the arts revealed both strengths and weaknesses. For example, the study found that students like to work with others and to engage in activities such as field trips, filmmaking, collecting, interviewing, and role playing. They like to be actively involved. "These are the things," Goodlad says, "which students reported doing least and which we observed infrequently.'' But he found that ''They were observed more frequently in the arts vocational education and physical education . . .''

These three subject areas were found to be ''a little less lecture- and textbook-oriented'' and to involve ''a little more participation of students in decisions affecting their learning, greater student enthusiasm, less time on instruction, and a little more variation in pedagogical procedures.'' And Goodlad states: ''It should not surprise us to learn that these three subjects consistently came out as the most liked in the eyes of the students sampled.''

While he found that students consistently rated the arts at all levels as ''more interesting and enjoyable than the academic subject fields,'' he also found that students rated them as ''relatively unimportant and easy.'' One can conjecture that the reason students believe the arts are less important than other subjects relates directly to the amount of standardized testing administered to them in those academic areas in comparison with the arts. The arts are also not required for college admission, and students are not slow to get that message. And it may well be, though Goodlad doesn't suggest it, that students perceive the arts as ''easy'' because they are interested and enjoying themselves and don't feel they are learning when, in fact, they are.

Throughout this book Goodlad expresses concern for a balance of studies and equal access to knowledge. He recommends that regional accrediting agencies specify a balanced curriculum in every school and for every high school student. He reasons that, ''If the minimum were 15% in English, 10% in each of mathematics, social studies, science, vocational education, the arts, and physical education, and 5% in foreign languages, a student still would have 20% of his or her time for following up special interests in any of these.'' In other words, this common curriculum would permit students ''to pursue areas of special interest (e.g., additional work in the arts) for the balance of time available.''

In a later chapter Goodlad makes additional recommendations about curricular balance:

If we can agree on the importance of the ''five fingers'' of human knowledge and organized experience—mathematics and science, literature and language, society and social studies, the arts, the vocations—then it remains to determine the desired balance, acceptable degrees of variance among them, and the time, if any, to be left completely free for individual choice.

Still further on, he offers a guiding question to determine curriculum: ''What *are* the significant areas of human knowledge and how can these be incorporated into a high school curriculum?'' Then he gives firm support to the arts as one of these significant areas:

It is important to point out, however, that the arts which tend to be underemphasized, have played a sig-

nificant role in history as a medium of expression and as a means of understanding human behavior and experience. To omit the arts in the secondary curriculum is to deprive the young of a major part of what is important in their education.

Among the recommendations he makes for improving the schools, Goodlad suggests ''the creation of centers designed to give long-term attention to research and development in school curricula and accompanying pedagogy.'' He mentions the arts specifically:

For example, there should be a center for research and development in arts education, not separately in the several divisions of the arts. The reason for this is that these centers must reflect the realities of finite resources (of time, for instance) in the schools. Elementary and secondary schools simply do not have the luxury of offering programs in music and dance to satisfy the expectations of specialists in these fields. What they need is a program likely to provide their students with some reasonable understanding, appreciation, and practice of the arts.

In his ''Coda,'' Goodlad notes that instruction in reading, writing, spelling, and arithmetic has long since been expanded to include introduction to social studies, science, the arts, and vocations. But, he says, ''there are inequities both among schools and within schools regarding students' opportunities to gain access to knowledge.'' He makes it clear that, in the task of reconstructing schools, the arts must retain a place of importance.

Notes

[1] John I. Goodlad, *A Place Called School: Prospects for the Future* (New York: McGraw-Hill, 1983), pp. 219-20.

[2] Ernest L. Boyer, *High School: A Report on Secondary Education in America* (New York: Harper & Row, Publishers, 1983), p. 98.

[3] *Op. cit.*, p. 220.

[4] *Ibid.*

[5] *A Nation at Risk: The Imperative for Educational Reform*, The National Commission on Excellence in Education (Washington, D.C.: U.S. Government Printing Office, 1983), p. 27.

[6] Reprinted with permission from *Academic Preparation for College: What Students Need to Know and Be Able to Do*, copyright 1983 by the College Entrance Examination Board, New York.

HOW TO OBTAIN THE REPORTS

Academic Preparation for College: What Students Need to Know and Be Able to Do, A Report of the Educational EQuality Project of the College Entrance Examination Board. Order #239200, College Board Publications, Dept. A35, Box 886, New York, N.Y. 10101.

Action for Excellence: A Comprehensive Plan to Improve Our Nation's Schools. The Task Force on Education for Economic Growth of the Education Commission of the States, 1860 Lincoln, #300, Denver, Colorado 80295.

A Nation At Risk: The Imperative for Educational Reform, A Report to the Nation and the Secretary of Education of the U.S. Department of Education by the National Commission on Excellence in Education, 1983. Stock no. 065-000-00177-2, Superintendent of Documents, U.S. Government Printing Office, Washington, D.C. 20402.

Boyer, Ernest L. *High School: A Report on Secondary Education in America*, by The Carnegie Foundation for the Advancement of Teaching (New York: Harper & Row, Publishers, 1983).

Goodlad John I. *A Place Called School: Prospects for the Future* (New York: McGraw-Hill Book Company, 1984).

Making the Grade: Report of the Twentieth Century Fund Task Force on Federal Elementary and Secondary Education Policy. The Twentieth Century Fund, 41 East 70th Street, New York, N.Y. 10021 (1983).

GARDNER WEBB COLLEGE LIBRARY

THE CONTRIBUTORS

Robert Alexander is founder and director of The Living Stage Theater Company, a venture of Arena Stage, Washington, D.C.

Arthur D. Efland is Professor of Art Education, The Ohio State University, Columbus.

Charles B. Fowler is a freelance writer and consultant in arts, Washington, D.C., as well as Education Editor of *Musical America/High Fidelity Magazine*. He is a former classroom music teacher.

Robert E. Gensemer is Associate Professor and Director of Graduate Studies, Department of Physical Education and Support Sciences, University of Denver.

Lee Hudson is Guest Artist at the Department of Theatre Arts, University of North Dakota.

Henry S. Kepner, Jr. is Professor of Curriculum and Instruction, and is responsible for computer and mathematics education, at the University of Wisconsin, Milwaukee.

Rita Kotter is head of the Fine Arts Center at Fairview High School, Boulder, Colorado.

Moira Logan is Associate Professor of Dance, The Ohio State University, Columbus.

Beverly Whitaker Long is Professor and Chair of the Department of Speech Communication, University of North Carolina, Chapel Hill.

Jon J. Murray is a teacher of art, Mamaroneck High School, New York.

Michael O'Hara is a Lecturer in Education, University of Ulster at Coleraine, Northern Ireland.

Sharon Rasor is a fine arts educator, Wright State University, Dayton, Ohio.

Rosina Lopez de Short is an art teacher at Pojoaque High School, Santa Fe, New Mexico.

David I. Steinberg teaches academics through music at Kingsbury Lab School, Washington, D.C.

Judith E. Traub is a reading specialist of the Junior High Program at Kingsbury Lab School, Washington, D.C.

Frederick B. Tuttle, Jr. is Director of Curriculum and Instruction for the Wareham Public Schools, Massachusetts and an educational consultant in gifted education and written composition. He is the author of five publications on gifted and talented education, and *Composition: A Media Approach*, published by NEA.

Yankelovich, Skelly and White, Inc., is a social and market research organization in New York.